A Theory of the Firm's Cost of Capital

How Debt Affects the Firm's Risk, Value,
Tax Rate and the Government's Tax Claim

A Theory of the Firm's Cost of Capital

How Debt Affects the Firm's Risk, Value,
Tax Rate and the Government's Tax Claim

Ramesh K S Rao

University of Texas at Austin, USA

Eric C Stevens

USA

NEW JERSEY · LONDON · SINGAPORE · BEIJING · SHANGHAI · HONG KONG · TAIPEI · CHENNAI

Published by

World Scientific Publishing Co. Pte. Ltd.

5 Toh Tuck Link, Singapore 596224

USA office: 27 Warren Street, Suite 401-402, Hackensack, NJ 07601

UK office: 57 Shelton Street, Covent Garden, London WC2H 9HE

Library of Congress Cataloging-in-Publication Data
Rao, Ramesh K. S.
    A theory of the firm's cost of capital : how debt affects the firm's risk,
value, tax rate, and the government's tax claim / by Ramesh K.S. Rao &
Eric C. Stevens.
      p. cm.
    Includes bibliographical references.
    ISBN-13 978-981-256-949-3 -- ISBN-10 981-256-949-9
     1. Corporations--Finance. 2. Capital costs. 3. Corporate debt. 4. Capital assets
pricing model. 5. Financial leverage. I. Stevens, Eric C., 1962–   . II. Title.

    HG4026.R366 2007
    338.6'04101--dc22

                                    2006052555

British Library Cataloguing-in-Publication Data
A catalogue record for this book is available from the British Library.

Typeset by Stallion Press
Email: enquiries@stallionpress.com

Printed in Singapore by World Scientific Printers (S) Pte Ltd

Preface

Modigliani and Miller's (MM) seminal analyses spawned two broad research strands in corporate finance, the first relating to the effects of leverage on the firm risk and cost of capital, and the second to the firm's optimal capital structure (mix of debt and equity). This book is concerned with the first, and it is a slightly expanded version of our paper that was published by the Berkeley Electronic Journals in Economic Analysis and Policy.[*]

Our original motivation for this research was the "pie-slicing" analogy that is the core intuition of modern corporate finance theory. In essence, the firm's investment decision determines the size of the economic pie that the firm creates, and debt and equity are simply two different claims on this pie. Thus, as MM argued, it does not matter, in frictionless capital markets, how this pie is sliced; the firm's capital structure is unimportant. When this intuition is extended to include corporate taxes, the size of the pie is determined by the firm's after-tax cash flows and, in this case, thanks to the government's

---

[*]Rao, RKS and EC Stevens (2006). The firm's cost of capital, its effective marginal tax rate, and the value of the government's tax claim. *Topics in Economic Analysis & Policy*, 6(1), Article 3, published by Berkeley Electronic Press, available at http://www.bepress.com/bejeap/topics/vol6/iss1/art3. This article is adapted here with permission.

subsidy of the firm's interest payments, maximizing debt becomes optimal.

With taxes, there are now three claimants to the economic pie—stockholders, bondholders and the tax authority. Thus, one should, in principle, be able to value the firm as the sum of the values of three claims. Although this intuition was well known, we did not see a satisfactory formal analysis of the "three claims view of the firm" with risky debt and corporate tax effects. The literature's focus was on "two claims models" of the firm. Our primary goal, thus, was to develop a theoretical framework that can identify how the value of the government's tax claim varies with corporate borrowing. In the analysis that is presented here, the value of the firm is consistent with the standard perspective that the firm's after-tax output is distributed between the debt and the equity, and also with the view that the pre-tax output is apportioned among three risky claims, with the tax authority being the third claimant.

As we worked on this research, it became clear that with risky debt and corporate taxes it is critical to understand how the risks of the firm's depreciation and the debt tax shields change with leverage. To our knowledge, the risk of the tax shields had not been adequately formalized in the research, and authors have relied on various *ad hoc* assumptions about the tax shields' risks. A second research goal, therefore, was to model how the tax shields' risks are affected by leverage.

The outcome of this effort, which is presented here, is a framework for better measuring the firm's cost of capital while, at the same time, identifying the marginal effects of debt policy on market values, risks, and expected rates of return. The ability of our model to capture several important economic interdependencies (e.g., between the borrowing rate and the tax shields) within a simple analytical framework allows us to illustrate the model with numerical examples and graphical illustration. As we discuss, the model can be used to generate better estimates of the firm's cost of capital and marginal corporate tax rates. In addition, it provides a conceptual framework for evaluating the implications of exogenous market forces (e.g., interest rates, tax laws, the market price of risk) on the firm's economic balance sheet and on the value of the government's claim on output, and thus may be useful for studies of tax and public policies.

We are grateful to the Berkeley Electronic Press for permission to reproduce our earlier paper in modified form. We also thank our spouses for their support, and the colleagues that have provided feedback on various drafts of the manuscript. Finally, we thank the staff of World Scientific, namely Juliet Lee, Venkatesh Sandhya, Chean Chian Cheong and Hooi-Yean Lee for their efforts at bringing this book into the present form.

Ramesh K. S. Rao
Austin, Texas, USA

Eric C. Stevens
Salt Lake City, Utah, USA

September 2006

Contents

List of Figures

List of Tables

Chapter I

Introduction

The cost of capital is perhaps the most fundamental and widely used concept in financial economics. Business managers and regulators routinely employ estimates of the firm's weighted average cost of capital ($WACC$) and the marginal tax rate (MTR) for investment decisions, rate regulation, restructuring activities, and bankruptcy valuation.[1] In economics, the cost of capital and the MTR are central to the research on tax policy, regulation, and welfare analysis.[2]

---

[1]The MTR is the expected effective tax rate on an incremental dollar of taxable income arising from debt financing, holding investment fixed, and is the sum of the products of the tax rates (tax payment divided by taxable income) in each state of nature multiplied by the relevant state probability. Fullerton (1984) provides a taxonomy of various definitions of the effective tax rate in economics. Also see Graham (1996b) and Graham and Lemmon (1998).

[2]Lau (2000, p. 3) notes that the cost of capital "is now a standard variable in the analysis of macroeconomics and of investment behavior at the firm, industry and economy-wide levels. It has also become a standard tool for the assessment of economic impacts of changes in tax policy. The concepts of the 'cost of capital' and its associated measure of a 'marginal tax rate' have generated a voluminous literature in the economics of taxation... The 'cost of capital' has been incorporated into both conventional macroeconomic models and intertemporal general equilibrium models of the impacts of tax policy."

A majority of firms use a single company-wide *WACC* for analyzing investments (Bierman, 1993; Graham and Harvey, 2001), and several private companies (e.g., Ibbotson Associates, Brattle Group) generate *WACC* and *MTR* estimates for external use. This book develops a theory of the firm's *WACC* and its *MTR* with risky debt and potentially redundant debt and non-debt tax shields.

The *WACC* and the *MTR* are endogenous to the firm's debt policy. The borrowing interest rate (coupon rate, r), the risks of the non-debt (depreciation) and debt (interest) tax shields, the *WACC*, and the *MTR* are intertwined, and they must be determined together. Increasing debt increases interest payments, not just because the firm is borrowing more, but also because creditors will require that each debt dollar pay a higher r, due to increased default risk. At the same time, increasing debt also increases the probability that some tax shields will be unusable (DeAngelo and Masulis, 1980; Mackie-Mason, 1990). The tax shields' risks and values depend on interactions between the debt and non-debt deductions (Zechner and Swoboda, 1986).[3] Thus a circularity arises—as debt increases and r changes, the tax shields and firm (debt plus equity) value change. This alters r, which, in turn, may change the tax shields' magnitudes and risks. Thus, even with a fixed statutory corporate tax rate, the *MTR* may be reduced. Since r reflects the tax shields' value, it influences and is, in turn, influenced by the *MTR*.

Prior research has noted, but not modeled, these interactions. This is because the related theory has developed along two broad research strands, each employing a different research strategy. First, capital structure research uses state-pricing to examine the combined value of the debt and equity. Second, cost of capital theory assumes riskless

---

[3]Bulow and Summers (1984) criticize the treatment of depreciation in the extant research, pointing out that it is important to recognize the stochastic nature of tax depreciation. They do not, however, explore the link between the risk of the deprecation tax shields and firm value, nor interdependencies between the depreciation and interest deductions.

debt (e.g., Hite, 1977) and uses capital asset pricing model ($CAPM$) pricing (default results in "kinked" equity payoffs, and this violates the $CAPM$'s assumptions).[4]

This research employs two innovations. First, we assume that priced risk is the standardized covariance of returns with an exogenous factor generating economy-wide shocks and that a single-factor version of the approximate arbitrage pricing theory (APT) holds (a later chapter elaborates). Second, to capture interdependencies between the tax shields' risks and the MTR, we determine r endogenously. Following the tradition in the cost of capital theory, we do not model bankruptcy costs. The model parameters can be estimated from historical data, and the theory thus implemented.

This research strategy provides better cost of capital estimates. We compare our results to standard textbook and industry cost of capital formulations that are derived from the riskless debt assumption. Our model also identifies the correct discount rate for valuing the tax shields and yields implications for estimation of firms' MTR. Collectively, our related $WACC$ and MTR findings have potentially important implications for low- and high-debt firms.

We also derive the firm's debt capacity—the maximum that the firm can borrow irrespective of the interest rate that it is willing to offer. Evidence indicates that acquiring external funds is not always easy (Graham and Harvey, 2001), and our model provides managers insights into the determinants of debt capacity. We find that debt capacity depends on characteristics of the firm's investment and on exogenous economic variables. An implication is that managers, to the extent that they can alter characteristics of their assets, can alter their debt capacity.

---

[4]The options approach (e.g., Galai and Masulis, 1976) admits kinked payoffs, but taxes pose technical problems. The difficulties associated with admitting interest tax shields in the options theory are discussed in, for example, Long (1974), Majd and Myers (1985), and Scholes and Wolfson (1992). These challenges are compounded with depreciation tax shields and, to simplify, continuous time models typically assume zero coupon debt and abstract from depreciation (e.g., Brennan and Schwartz, 1978; Ross, 1987; Leland, 1994).

The result that the firm maximizes borrowing with riskless debt and tax benefits (and no bankruptcy costs) is the classic result of Modigliani and Miller (MM, 1963). We examine how this result changes with risky debt and risky tax shields. As it turns out, and somewhat surprisingly, we find that the firm will still optimally maximize debt; the MM all-debt result is preserved.

Finally, our methodology allows us to value the government's (tax) claim across alternative debt levels. We specify numerically how policy variables (tax rate, tax rules, and the riskless rate) affect the market values of both the private (debt and equity) and public (tax) claims, thus providing a potentially useful conceptual framework for tax and interest policy debates.[5]

The book has eight chapters. Chapter II describes our accounting, tax, and pricing assumptions. Chapter III describes our distributional assumptions, initially a joint binomial assumption ($2 \times 2 = 4$ states) that yields analytical expressions for the risks and the costs of capital. The firm's realized cash flows are two firm-states, and the return on the factor generating economy-wide shocks takes on two macro-states. We consider all possible tax and default/solvency states in this single-period four-state economy and identify the risks of the tax shields and of the firm. Chapter IV presents a four-step solution procedure that yields the cost of capital. Chapter V discusses results of the binomial model and provides the intuition for our findings. It also derives the firm's debt capacity. Chapter VI generalizes the model to $s \times s$ states. Chapter VII contains numerical illustrations. The final chapter closes. Appendix A addresses technical issues. Given the exogenous policy variables, Appendix B illustrates the effect of each marginal debt dollar on the firm's economic balance sheet, its *WACC*, and the *MTR*.

---

[5] As is well known, current theory does not lend itself to such numerical specification. Copeland (2002) argues that for corporate finance theory to be useful to managers, it is important to be able to illustrate the theory with a complete numerical example.

Chapter II

Model Setting

An entrepreneur/owner sets up the firm/project at $t = 0$ and dismantles it at $t = 1$.[6] The capital markets are perfect (frictionless) except for corporate taxes. An investment in an amount A represents all assets (physical or otherwise, such as licenses or patents) required to generate an uncertain end-of-period output. The owner runs the firm to maximize personal wealth and, for this purpose, considers debt financing. Operations yield a $t = 1$ net output $\tilde{X}$ (gross margin on a cash flow basis plus the liquidation value of A). Output $\tilde{X}$ is apportioned among the tax authority, creditors (if debt is used), and equity holders. As noted, we abstract from bankruptcy costs. To be viable, and consistent with limited liability, we assume the firm covers its variable costs so that $\tilde{X}$ is nonnegative with probability

---

[6]The research routinely assumes that the firm is a perpetuity. This makes the analysis tractable, but it obscures the tax effects of default and necessitates out-of-model assumptions about the tax shields' risks. Out-of-model tax shield risk assumptions also affect economic linkages between the *MTR* and the *WACC*.

density $f_{\tilde{X}}$. The pre-tax net present value of the investment plan is:

$$NPV_A = V_X - A, \tag{1}$$

where V_X is the risk-adjusted present value of $\tilde{X}$. The asset can be
fully or partially financed by the owner at $t = 0$. The owner provides
E_0 of initial equity ($0 < E_0 \leqslant A$) and receives a $t = 1$ equity cash flow
with a $t = 0$ market value of V_E. For a firm without debt, $E_0 = A$.
If $E_0 < A$, the firm borrows $A - E_0$ to finance A, and it may borrow
more than A. The firm issues coupon debt with face value D, agreeing
to pay interest at a rate r and to repay principal at $t = 1$. The value of
the debt claim is V_D. We assume par debt, so that $D = V_D$. The value
of the tax claim is V_T. The owner's $t = 0$ wealth increase from setting
up the firm is the difference between the value of his/her holdings and
his/her contributed capital, $\Delta W = V_E - E_0$. When $D > A$, he/she
may pay himself/herself a $t = 0$ dividend DIV_0 equal to his/her
wealth increase.[7] Creditors examine the investment plan and general
economic variables and specify the firm's borrowing schedule—the
rates r that they require for different borrowing amounts, and the
maximum they will lend (debt capacity). The interest rate is thus
endogenous.

The tax code specifies the corporate tax rate and other tax rules.
Our accounting setup is similar to that of Green and Talmor (1985)
and Talmor *et al.* (1985), but without personal taxes. The "interest
first" doctrine applies for payments to creditors in default (Talmor
et al., 1985; Zechner and Swoboda, 1986). The initial investment A is
fully depreciable for tax purposes at $t = 1$. The tax rate on corporate
income is T. This is also the tax rate on the capital gain on the $t = 1$

---

[7]This assumption is consistent with the standard capital structure literature.
MM (1958, 1963) showed that the firm can borrow "up to firm value"—which, by
definition, is the market value of A plus the firm's economic rents (NPV). Since
cash has no positive role in the firm valuation theory, the owners can withdraw all
cash in excess of A (i.e., the rents) as an immediate dividend, and bondholders
will not object. They are fully aware of this possibility; the firm's future cash
flows protect their claims, and the coupon rate, r, reflects this possibility.

liquidation value of A. The interest expense, rD, is tax deductible (the principal, D, is not).[8] The US tax code allows firms to deduct interest even on borrowing that exceeds A. Depreciation is senior to the interest deduction. To preclude negative taxes, we assume that taxes are paid only if taxable income is positive. The depreciation and the debt tax shield are denoted by subscripts NTS and DTS and their market values by V_{NTS} and V_{DTS}, respectively.

The firm is financially solvent when output $\tilde{X}$ is sufficient to fully pay interest and repay principal, that is, when $\tilde{X} - T \cdot MAX$ $[\tilde{X} - rD - A, \ 0] \geqslant D(1 + r)$. The "just solvent" or financial break-even level of output, X^*, is defined by $X^* - MAX[T(X^* - rD - A), \ 0] = D(1 + r)$. Depending on the debt amount, there are two expressions for X^*:

$$X^* = \begin{cases} D(1 + r), & \text{if } D \leqslant A, \\ \dfrac{D(1 + r) - (rD + A)T}{1 - T}, & \text{if } D > A. \end{cases} \tag{2}$$

If $D \leqslant A$, the firm may be solvent even with negative taxable income. If $D > A$, the firm is solvent only if taxable income is positive.[9]

Table 1 illustrates tax shield utilization and debt default/solvency possibilities for different levels of $\tilde{X}$, D, and A. The extent to which the tax shields are utilized depends on the magnitudes of A, the borrowing amount D, the coupon rate r, the financial breakeven level of output X^*, and the output realization $\tilde{X}$.

Let $\tilde{\Phi}_i$ be the $t = 1$ cash flow to i. We use the following notation: $\tilde{\Phi}_{DTS}$ is the cash flow from the debt tax shield, $\tilde{\Phi}_{NTS}$ is the cash

---

[8]The working assumption that both interest and principal are tax deductible (e.g., DeAngelo and Masulis, 1980; Kraus and Litzenberger, 1973; MM, 1963; Rubinstein, 1973; Turnbull, 1979; Ross, 1985, 1987) leads to internal inconsistencies (see Talmor *et al.*, 1985; Baron, 1975).

[9]If solvency occurs when taxable income is negative, $T(X^* - rD - A) \leqslant 0 \Rightarrow$ $X^* \leqslant rD + A$, and, since $X^* = D(1 + r)$, $D(1 + r) \leqslant rD + A \Rightarrow D \leqslant A$. If solvency occurs when taxable income is positive, $T(X^* - rD - A) > 0 \Rightarrow X^* > Dr + A$, and since $X^* = \frac{D(1+r)-(rD+A)T}{1-T}$, $\frac{D(1+r)-(rD+A)T}{1-T} > rD + A$, which implies $D > A$.

Table 1. Tax shield use, tax status, and financial solvency for different levels of output $\tilde{X}$ and of debt D in relation to assets A.

$X^* \leqslant A:$

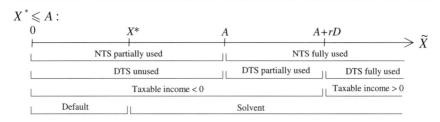

$D \leqslant A < X^*:$

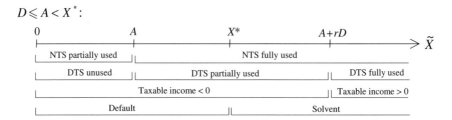

$A < D:$

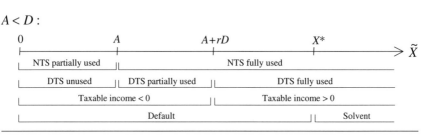

Note: When $X^* \leqslant A$ or $D \leqslant A < X^*$, $D \leqslant A$ and hence $X^* = D(1 + r)$, by Equation (2). When $A < D$ we have $X^* = \frac{D(1+r) - (rD + A)T}{1 - T}$.

flow from the non-debt (depreciation) tax shield, $\tilde{\Phi}_{TTS}$ is the cash flow from total tax shields, $\tilde{\Phi}_T$ is the cash flow to the tax claimant, $\tilde{\Phi}_D$ is the cash flow to the debt holders, $\tilde{\Phi}_E$ is the cash flow to equity, and $\tilde{\Phi}_{D+E}$ is the cash flow to the levered firm (debt plus levered equity). Table 2 defines payouts from the tax shields and to the various claimants. Since these output apportionment formulas are well known, we do not discuss them further. Figure 1 provides a graphical representation of the output apportionment formulas.

Table 2. Output apportionment for tax shields and claims.

Depreciation tax shield	$\tilde{\Phi}_{NTS} = MIN\left[\tilde{X}T, AT\right]$
Debt tax shield	$\tilde{\Phi}_{DTS} = MAX\left[0, MIN\left[(\tilde{X} - A)T, rDT\right]\right]$
Total tax shield	$\tilde{\Phi}_{TTS} = MIN\left[\tilde{X}T, (A + rD)T\right]$
Tax claim	$\tilde{\Phi}_T = MAX\left[0, (\tilde{X} - A - rD)T\right]$
Debt	$\tilde{\Phi}_D = \begin{cases} D \leqslant A : MIN\left[\tilde{X}, X^*\right] \\ D > A : MIN\left[\tilde{X}, \tilde{X}(1-T) + (A + rD)T, D(1 + r)\right] \end{cases}$
Equity	$\tilde{\Phi}_E = \begin{cases} D \leqslant A : MAX\left[0, MIN\left[\tilde{X} - X^*, \tilde{X}(1-T) + AT - D(1 + r(1 - T))\right]\right] \\ D > A : MAX\left[0, (\tilde{X} - X^*)(1 - T)\right] \end{cases}$
The firm	$\tilde{\Phi}_{D+E} = MIN\left[\tilde{X}, \tilde{X}(1-T) + (A + rD)T\right]$

Net output

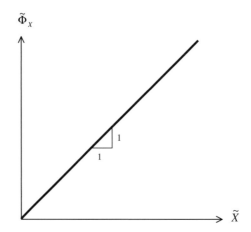

Depreciation tax shield

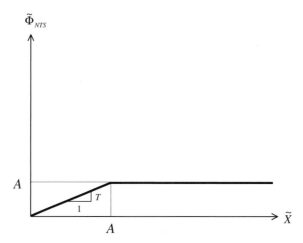

Figure 1. Output apportionment diagrams for the tax shields and claims (using Table 2).

Debt tax shield

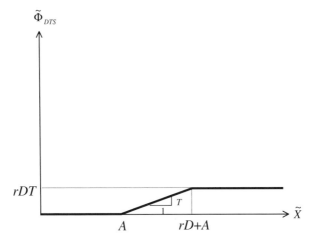

Total tax shield

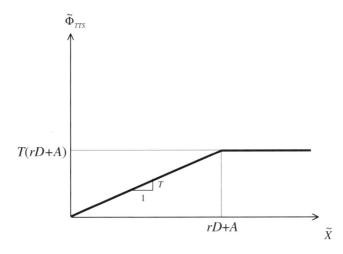

Figure 1.   (*Continued*)

Tax claim

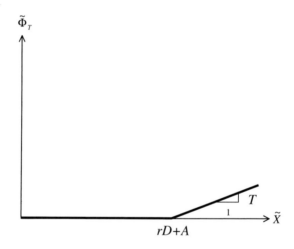

Figure 1.   (*Continued*)

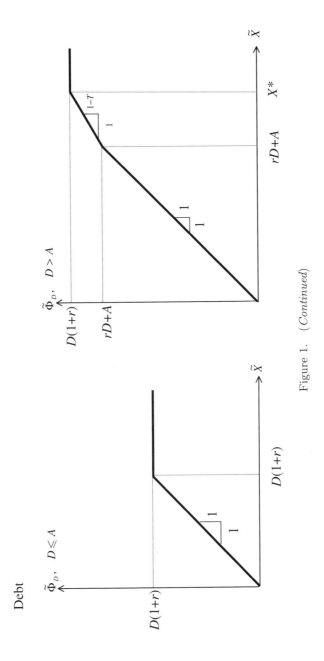

Figure 1. (*Continued*)

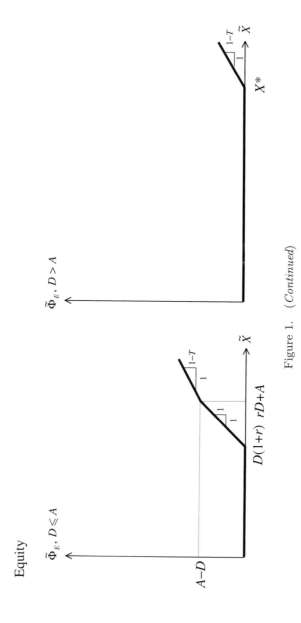

Figure 1. (*Continued*)

The firm

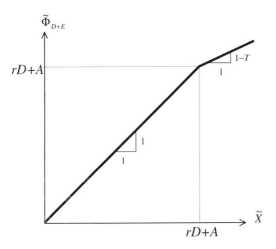

Figure 1.   (*Continued*)

The apportionment formulas in Table 2 can be reinterpreted using option payoff language. The "underlying asset" for all claims is net output, $\tilde{X}$ (not the firm's assets). For each additional dollar of $\tilde{X}$ in the range $0 < \tilde{X} < A$, the depreciation tax shield (NTS) provides a tax savings of T dollars. When $A < \tilde{X}$, the depreciation tax shield is fully utilized and the cash flow from it is AT. The depreciation tax shield is equivalent to a long position in a riskless discount bond with principal TA plus a short position in $1 - T$ put options with strike price A. The debt tax shield (DTS) is a bull spread on $\tilde{X}$, or long T call options with strike price A and short T call options with strike price $rD + A$. Because depreciation is deducted first, the debt tax shield goes unused if $\tilde{X} < A$; for each additional dollar of $\tilde{X}$ in the range $A < \tilde{X} < rD + A$, the debt tax shield provides a tax savings of T dollars. For $rD + A < \tilde{X}$, the debt tax shield is fully utilized, generating tax savings of rDT. The debt claim is the familiar riskless bond plus short put on $\tilde{X}$ with strike price $D(1 + r)$, but only when $D \leqslant A$. When $D > A$, the debt claim is a long position in $\tilde{X}$, short T call options with strike price $rD + A$ (total deductions) and short $1 - T$ call options with strike price X^*. The equity claim is the familiar long position in $1 - T$ call options on $\tilde{X}$ with strike price X^*, but only when $D > A$. When $D \leqslant A$, the equity claim is a long call option on $\tilde{X}$ with strike price $D(1 + r)$ plus a short position in T call options on $\tilde{X}$ with strike price $rD + A$. The payoff to the firm $(D + E)$ is equivalent to a long position in $\tilde{X}$ plus short T call options on $\tilde{X}$ with strike price $rD + A$.

MM (1958, 1963) showed that if the firm, assumed to be a perpetuity, chooses to finance its investments with default-free debt, the tax deductibility of interest lowers the after-tax cost of debt, and hence the firm's $WACC$. To estimate the cost of capital, the early research (Hamada, 1969; Rubinstein, 1973; Kim, 1978) extended the MM analyses to the single-period $CAPM$. However, the $CAPM$ cannot be used if the debt is risky (Gonzales *et al.*, 1977). If the firm can default on its debt, the equity payoffs become "kinked" (piecewise linear) and thus inadmissible in the pricing theory. The options approach, as noted, does not adequately handle tax effects. Thus, neither the $CAPM$ nor the options theory is adequate for estimating the after-tax cost of capital for the (typical) firm with risky and potentially redundant debt and non-debt tax shields. For this reason, as we subsequently discuss, we invoke the approximate APT.[10]

The economy has n traded assets. The linear projection of asset returns onto random variable $\tilde{e}$ is:

$$\underset{n\times1}{\tilde{R}} = E\left(\underset{n\times1}{\tilde{R}}\right) + \underset{n\times1}{\beta} \cdot \underset{1\times1}{\tilde{e}} + \underset{n\times1}{\tilde{\varepsilon}}, \tag{3}$$

where $\tilde{R}$ is the asset returns vector, $\tilde{e}$ is a pervasive, economy-wide risk factor, β is the vector of asset sensitivities to $\tilde{e}$, $\tilde{\varepsilon}$ is the idiosyncratic returns vector, and $E(\tilde{e}) = E(\tilde{\varepsilon}) = E(\tilde{e}\tilde{\varepsilon}') = 0$ (this holds automatically when asset returns are projected linearly onto random variable $\tilde{e}$). The random variables $\tilde{e}$ and $\tilde{\varepsilon}$ are assumed to have finite variance. The covariance matrix of returns is

$$\underset{n\times n}{\sum} = \beta \cdot E\left(\tilde{e}^2\right) \cdot \beta' + E(\tilde{\varepsilon} \cdot \tilde{\varepsilon}'). \tag{4}$$

The n assets include $m \times k$ corporate claims, where m is the number of firms and k is the number of distinct types of traded corporate claims. We assume k is small relative to m and that m

---

[10]The capital structure research (e.g., DeAngelo and Masulis, 1980; Talmor *et al.*, 1985; Ross, 1985; Dammon and Senbet, 1988; Lewis, 1990; Mauer and Triantis, 1994) relies on the state-pricing approach. These papers examine the (combined) value of the debt and equity claims, taking care to correctly model the payoffs arising from default and corporate taxes. Asset values are the expectation (with respect to martingale probabilities) of cash flows discounted at the riskless rate. The tax shields' risks and the firm's cost of capital are not central to this literature, and this research cannot identify the marginal effects of debt financing on the risks and values of the firm's claims. The cost of capital research, on the other hand, uses $CAPM$ pricing to generate risk-return metrics. Asset values are the expectation of cash flows (with respect to statistical probabilities) capitalized at the appropriate risk-adjusted discount rate. However, computing covariance with kinked payoffs is difficult, and these studies fail to model the payoffs precisely.

is small relative to n ($k \ll m \ll n$). Since the claims on the output of a particular firm are deterministic functions of its output, the idiosyncratic returns on these claims tend to be highly correlated. The idiosyncratic returns matrix $E(\tilde{\varepsilon} \cdot \tilde{\varepsilon}')$ is thus non-diagonal, and exact APT pricing (Ross, 1976) is precluded. Chamberlain and Rothschild (CR, 1983) show that approximate APT pricing is valid in this case, provided the idiosyncratic returns correlations are sufficiently small. Thus, kinked payoffs are admissible. (Also see Connor and Korazcyk, 1993.)

We assume the CR conditions on the eigenvalues of $\sum$ as $n \to \infty$ hold, namely, that $\sum$ has a single divergent eigenvalue as $n \to \infty$. This means a single factor is pervasive, and that idiosyncratic returns are diversifiable in the sense of CR (1983). Our assumption that $k \ll m \ll n$ justifies this. The approximate APT pricing expression is:

$$E(\tilde{R}_i) \approx r_z + \beta_i \cdot (E(\tilde{r}_e - r_z), \tag{5}$$

where $E(\tilde{r}_e)$ is the expected return on risk factor "e," and r_z is the expected return on the zero-beta asset. We assume markets price all assets (including corporate claims) according to Equation (5), with equality. The existence of non-traded assets (e.g., tax shields, the tax claim) is permissible in the linear factor framework, and the assumptions regarding the return generating process apply only to the traded assets (Grinblatt and Titman, 1983, 1985). The returns beta (or priced risk) of asset i is:

$$\beta_i = COV(\tilde{R}_i, \tilde{r}_e)(VAR(\tilde{r}_e))^{-1}, \tag{6}$$

and the cash flow beta of asset i is:

$$\beta_i = COV(\tilde{\Phi}_i, \tilde{r}_e) \cdot (VAR(\tilde{r}_e))^{-1} = \beta_i \cdot V_i, \tag{7}$$

where V_i is the risk-adjusted present value of i:

$$V_i = \frac{E(\tilde{\Phi}_i)}{1 + E(\tilde{R}_i)} = \frac{E(\tilde{\Phi}_i) - \beta_i \cdot (E(\tilde{r}_e) - r_z)}{1 + r_z}. \tag{8}$$

Chapter III

Distributional Assumptions

We assume four states of nature at $t = 1$, where the cash flow on asset i, $\tilde{\Phi}_i$, and the return on the priced risk factor $\tilde{r}_e$ have joint binomial probability distribution $f_{\tilde{\Phi}_i, \tilde{r}_e}$ with joint probability matrix $\underset{2 \times 2}{\mathbf{P}}$: [11]

$$
\begin{array}{c c}
 & \begin{array}{cc} r_{e,o} & r_{e,p} \end{array} \\
\begin{array}{c} \Phi_{i,o} \\ \Phi_{i,p} \end{array} & \boxed{\begin{array}{cc} \mathrm{p_{oo}} & \mathrm{p_{op}} \\ \mathrm{p_{po}} & \mathrm{p_{pp}} \end{array}} \begin{array}{c} \mathrm{P_o} \\ \mathrm{P_p} \end{array} \\
 & \begin{array}{cc} \mathrm{P_{e,o}} & \mathrm{P_{e,p}} \end{array}
\end{array} \tag{9}
$$

---

[11] A similar enumeration for an $s \times s$ model ($s > 2$) would yield an unmanageably large number of cases, and, in the interest of tractability we do not address this here. We later generalize the framework to the $s \times s$ ("joint s-nomial") setting, but use numerical methods to compute the debt coupon rate.

Subscripts "o" and "p" denote optimistic and pessimistic states.[12] The statistical (not risk-neutral) probabilities are p_{oo}, p_{op}, p_{po}, and p_{pp}. If historical data on $\tilde{\Phi}_i$ and $\tilde{r}_e$ are available, the parameters p_{oo}, p_{op}, p_{po}, p_{pp}, $\Phi_{i,o}$ $\Phi_{i,p}$, $r_{e,o}$, and $r_{e,p}$ can be estimated using maximum likelihood methods. An alternative estimation strategy is to iterate on p_{oo}, p_{op}, p_{po}, p_{pp}, $\Phi_{i,o}$, $\Phi_{i,p}$, $r_{e,o}$, and $r_{e,p}$ to produce desired values of $E(\tilde{\Phi}_i)$, $E(\tilde{r}_e)$, $VAR(\tilde{\Phi}_i)$, $VAR(\tilde{r}_e)$, and $COV(\tilde{\Phi}_i, \tilde{r}_e)$. The cash flow beta of asset i is[13]:

$$\mathbf{B}_i = (\tilde{\Phi}_{i,o} - \Phi_{i,p}) \cdot \frac{\theta_i}{r_{e,o} - r_{e,p}}, \quad \text{where } \theta_i = \frac{p_{oo}p_{pp} - p_{op}p_{po}}{P_{e,o}P_{e,p}}. \quad (10)$$

Equation (10) is crucial for our results since it simplifies the valuation of kinked payoffs. Equation (8) and (10) yield a risk-neutral valuation (RNV) expression for asset i:

$$V_i = \frac{\pi_i \cdot \Phi_{i,o} + (1 - \pi_i) \cdot \Phi_{i,p}}{1 + r_z}, \quad \text{where } \pi_i = P_o - \frac{\theta_i \cdot (E(\tilde{r}_e) - r_z)}{r_{e,o} - r_{e,p}}. \quad (11)$$

The state "o" risk-neutral probability for asset i is π_i.[14] Dividing the cash flow beta in Equation (10) by the value of asset i in Equation (11) yields the returns beta of asset i:

$$\beta_i = \frac{\Phi_{i,o} - \Phi_{i,p}}{V_i} \cdot \frac{\theta_i}{r_{e,o} - r_{e,p}} = \frac{\Phi_{i,o} - \Phi_{i,p}}{\pi_i \cdot \Phi_{i,o} + (1 - \pi_i) \cdot \Phi_{i,p}} \cdot \frac{\theta_i \cdot (1 + r_z)}{r_{e,o} - r_{e,p}}. \quad (12)$$

---

[12]We assume $\Phi_{i,p} \leqslant \Phi_{i,o}$, $r_{e,p} < r_z < E(\tilde{r}_e) < r_{e,o}$, $0 < r_z$, $0 \leqslant p_{ij} \leqslant 1$, $P_{e,o} = p_{oo} + p_{po}$, $P_{e,p} = p_{op} + p_{pp}$, $P_o = p_{oo} + p_{op}$, $P_p = p_{po} + p_{pp}$, $P_{e,o} + P_{e,p} = 1$, $P_o + P_p = 1$, $0 < P_{e,p}$, and $0 < P_{e,o}$.

[13]$\mathbf{B}_i = \frac{COV(\tilde{\Phi}_i \tilde{r}_e)}{VAR(\tilde{r}_e)} = \frac{(p_{oo}p_{pp} - p_{op}p_{po})(\Phi_{i,o} - \Phi_{i,p})(r_{e,o} - r_{e,p})}{P_{e,o}P_{e,p}(r_{e,o} - r_{e,p})^2} = \theta_i \cdot \frac{\Phi_{i,o} - \Phi_{i,p}}{r_{e,o} - r_{e,p}}$.

[14]Since π_i can be written as

$$\pi_i = \frac{1}{r_{e,o} - r_{e,p}} \cdot \left(\frac{p_{op}}{P_{e,p}} (r_{e,o} - r_z) + \frac{p_{oo}}{P_{e,o}} (r_z - r_{e,p}) \right),$$

we have $0 < \pi_i < 1$ by inspection.

The risk adjustment to asset i's state "o" probability of occurrence, P_o, is $\frac{\theta_i \cdot (E(\tilde{r}_e) - r_z)}{r_{e,o} - r_{e,p}}$.[15] The probability π_i can be used to value asset i and any other asset that has the same joint binomial probability matrix as asset i, such as a contingent claim on asset i. The underlying asset for all corporate claims is $\tilde{X}$, and since these claims have the same joint binomial probability matrix $\mathbf{P}$, they can all be valued using θ_x or π_x.

---

[15] θ_i is akin to the correlation between $\tilde{\Phi}_i$ and the return on the priced risk factor $\tilde{r}_e$:

$$CORR(\tilde{\Phi}_i, \tilde{r}_e) = \frac{P_{po}P_{pp} - P_{op}P_{po}}{\sqrt{P_o P_p P_{e,o} P_{e,p}}}.$$

Note that sign $\{\theta_i\}$ = sign$\{CORR(\tilde{\Phi}_i, \tilde{r}_e)\}$ = sign $\{\mathbf{B}_i\}$. If $\mathbf{P}$ is symmetric about either diagonal, then $\sqrt{P_o P_p P_{e,o} P_{e,p}} = P_{e,o} P_{e,p}$ and $\theta_i = CORR(\tilde{\Phi}_i, \tilde{r}_e)$.

Chapter IV

Model Solution Procedure

The firm's cost of capital and the market value of all claims on the firm's output are determined in four steps. In this chapter we focus on the procedure by which the model is solved. The numerical examples in a later chapter implement this solution methodology. An interpretation of these results is deferred to the next chapter.

Step 1. The Relevant Tax States

The first step involves identification of the relevant tax states. Table 1 shows that the extent to which the tax shields are utilized depends on the magnitude of the depreciable assets A, the distribution of the output $\tilde{X}$, the breakeven output level X^* [from Equation (2)], D, and r. The tax states also depend on the borrowing rate, and this rate, in turn, defines the tax states. This highlights the importance of endogenizing r.

Given the assumed tax rules, Table 2 shows how the cash flows are apportioned among the various claims. Note that the cash flows to the debt and equity depend, because of the tax treatment of interest and depreciation, on the relation between the amount borrowed, D, and the value of the firm's physical assets, A.

Table 3 enumerates all possible distributions of binomial $\tilde{X}$ across all tax, default/solvency and tax shield utilization/redundancy situations. The columns in Table 3 indicate where X_o falls and the rows indicate where X_p falls. In every case $\tilde{X}$ must exceed X^* at least in state "o" $(= X_o)$ so that the debt can be issued at par. As seen from this table, there are 20 possible cases. Each pricing case in Table 3 implies a corresponding risk for the tax shields, the debt, the firm, and the tax claim, in Table A.1.

It is not easy to generalize the implications of the pricing cases in Table 3. The relevant pricing case depends on the magnitudes of the borrowing rate, the investment's pre-tax NPV, and the value of the tax shields. Appendix A.1 shows that in cases 1–8 NPV_A may be positive or negative, in cases 9–12 it is strictly positive, and in cases 13–20 it is strictly negative.

Thus, our analysis accommodates both positive and negative NPV firms. This is interesting because it establishes an economic linkage between an investment's economic viability and the cost of capital. The reader will recognize that the standard cost of capital theory, with its focus on firm value, is silent about the significance of the firm's pre-tax NPV. Our interest in this research is not on these cases *per se*; they serve only to ensure that the resultant cost of capital theory is consistent in every one of these cases.

It is useful to illustrate, with reference to a specific situation, how Table 3 is used in developing our cost of capital results. Consider, for example, the situation where $A < D$. Four cases are possible:

Table 3. Pricing cases for the 2×2 model. Enumerates possible distributions of $\tilde{X} = \{X_\mathrm{p}, X_\mathrm{o}\}$ across the tax and solvency states in Table 1. The rows depict X_p, the columns X_o. Twenty cases exist. The par yield (see Table 5 for r_z, r_D, and r_{11}), tax shield risk status, and the sign of NPV_A (see Appendix A.1) are indicated for each case.

	$X^* \leqslant X_\mathrm{o} \leqslant A$	$A < X_\mathrm{o} \leqslant A + rD$	$A + rD < X_\mathrm{o}$
$X^* \leqslant A$:			1: r_D, NTS, DTS, $NPV_{A+/-}$
$X_\mathrm{p} < X^*$	19: r_D, NTS, DTSW, NPV_{A-}	13: r_D, NTS, DTS, NPV_{A-}	2: r_z, NTS, DTS, $NPV_{A+/-}$
$X^* \leqslant X_\mathrm{p} \leqslant A$	20: r_z, NTS, DTSW, NPV_{A-}	14: r_z, NTS, DTS, NPV_{A-}	3: r_z, DTS, $NPV_{A+/-}$
$A < X_\mathrm{p} \leqslant A + rD$		15: r_z, DTS, NPV_{A-}	4: r_z, $NPV_{A+/-}$
$A + rD < X_\mathrm{p}$			
	$X^* \leqslant X_\mathrm{o} \leqslant A + rD$		$A + rD < X_\mathrm{o}$
$D \leqslant A < X^*$:			5: r_D, NTS, DTS, $NPV_{A+/-}$
$X_\mathrm{p} \leqslant A$	16: r_D, NTS, DTS, NPV_{A-}		6: r_D, DTS, $NPV_{A+/-}$
$A < X_\mathrm{p} < X^*$	17: r_D, DTS, NPV_{A-}		7: r_z, DTS, $NPV_{A+/-}$
$X^* \leqslant X_\mathrm{p} \leqslant A + rD$	18: r_z, DTS, NPV_{A-}		8: r_z, $NPV_{A+/-}$
$A + rD < X_\mathrm{p}$			
	$X^* \leqslant X_\mathrm{o}$		
$A < D$:			9: r_D, NTS, DTS, NPV_{A+}
$X_\mathrm{p} \leqslant A$			10: r_D, DTS, NPV_{A+}
$A < X_\mathrm{p} \leqslant A + rD$			11: r_{11}, NPV_{A+}
$A + rD < X_p < X^*$			12: r_z, NPV_{A+}
$X^* \leqslant X_\mathrm{p}$			

r_z: Debt is riskless and par yield $= r_z$; r_D: Debt is risky and par yield $= r_D$; r_{11}: Debt is risky and par yield $= r_{11}$; NTS: Depreciation (non-debt) tax shield is risky; DTS: Debt tax shield is risky; DTSW: Debt tax shield is worthless; NPV_{A+}: NPV_A is positive; NPV_{A-}: NPV_A is negative or zero; $NPV_{A+/-}$: Sign of NPV_A may be positive or negative.

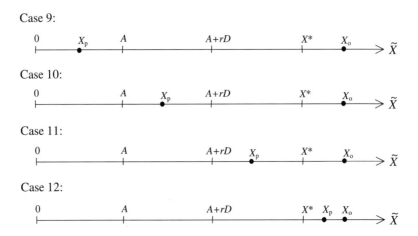

Case 9:

Case 10:

Case 11:

Case 12:

In state of nature "o," X_o is sufficiently large in cases 9–12 that all tax shields are utilized, taxes are paid, and debt principal is fully repaid. In state of nature "p," X_p may fall in one of four possible ranges. In case 9, $X_p \leqslant A$, the depreciation deduction is partially unused, and the debt tax shield is fully redundant (completely unused). In case 10, the depreciation deduction is fully taken while the debt tax shield is partially unused. In case 11, all tax shields are fully utilized and the firm pays taxes, but after-tax cash flow is insufficient to fully repay debt principal. In case 12, all tax shields are fully utilized, the firm pays taxes, and after-tax funds are sufficient to fully repay creditors. The debt is riskless in case 12, since creditors are fully paid in both states of nature. The debt is risky in cases 9–11, since state "p" entails partial default on interest or principal or on both. The depreciation tax shield is riskless in cases 10–12, since the cash flow from the depreciation deduction is a constant AT in both states of nature (see $\tilde{\Phi}_{NTS}$ in Table 2). In case 9, cash flow from the depreciation tax shield is AT in state "o" but only $X_p T < AT$ in state "p." Similarly, the debt tax shield is riskless in cases 11 and 12, since it provides a tax shield of rDT in both states of nature; in cases 9 and 10 it is risky, since in state of nature "p" the cash flow from the debt tax shield is $(X_p - A)T < rDT$ (case 10) or zero (case 9). As noted earlier, NPV_A is positive in cases 9–12 and is zero or negative in cases 13–20. In cases 1–8, NPV_A may be positive or negative.

Now consider, for purposes of illustration, the depreciation tax shield. Table 4 illustrates the risk and valuation calculations for the depreciation tax shield. First, cash flow from the depreciation deduction ($\tilde{\Phi}_{NTS}$) is computed for states of nature "o" and "p" for each of the 20 pricing cases in Table 3. Cases are combined where cash flows are identical. Three groups of cases exist for the depreciation tax shield. In the first group (cases 1, 2, 5, 9, 13, 14, and 16) the depreciation deduction is partially unused in state of nature "p," and is risky. In the second group (cases 3, 4, 6–8, 10–12, 15, 17, and 18) the depreciation shield is a (riskless) constant AT in both states. In the third group (cases 19 and 20) the depreciation deduction is partly unused in both states, and is risky, if $X_p < X_o$.

The value of the non-debt tax shield (V_{NTS}) is computed for each group of cases using the RNV expression (11). Finally, Equation (12) yields the returns beta (β_{NTS}) for each group of cases. The risk of the depreciation tax shields is unaffected by borrowing (see β_{NTS} in Table A.1). This is a direct implication of the assumption that depreciation is senior to the interest deduction.

Step 2. Determine the Par Yield

Since r affects the cash flows to the tax authority and to equity, it must be computed before valuing the debt tax shield, the tax claim, and the equity claim. The debt is valued in a manner similar to the depreciation tax shield except that r must be simultaneously computed such that the debt is fairly priced at par. We next discuss details of how the debt is priced and r determined.

Creditors examine the investment plan $(A, f_{\tilde{\Phi}_X}, \tilde{r}_c)$, the proposed borrowing level D, and general economic conditions (π_X, r_z) to assess the risk of the $t = 1$ debt cash flow, $\tilde{\Phi}_D$. They demand a coupon rate that equates their expected return with their opportunity cost $[E(\tilde{R}_D) = k_D]$ so that $V_D = D$. The par yield is the coupon rate r

Table 4. Illustration of valuation of the depreciation tax shield. From Table 2, output apportionment formula for depreciation tax shield is $\tilde{\Phi}_{NTS} = MIN[\tilde{X}T, AT]$.

Cases	$\tilde{\Phi}_{NTS,\mathrm{o}} = MIN[\tilde{X}_\mathrm{o}T, AT]$	$\tilde{\Phi}_{NTS,\mathrm{p}} = MIN[\tilde{X}_\mathrm{p}T, AT]$

$\tilde{\Phi}_{NTS}$ by pricing case (Table 3) and by state of nature ("o," "p")

Cases	$\tilde{\Phi}_{NTS,\mathrm{o}}$	$\tilde{\Phi}_{NTS,\mathrm{p}}$
1, 2, 5, 9, 13, 14, 16	AT	$X_\mathrm{p}T$
3, 4, 6–8, 10–12, 15, 17, 18	AT	AT
19, 20	$X_\mathrm{o}T$	$X_\mathrm{p}T$

$$\text{Cases} \qquad V_{NTS} = \frac{E^{\pi_X}(\tilde{\Phi}_{NTS})}{1+r_z} = \frac{E^{\pi_X} MIN[\tilde{X}T, AT]}{1+r_z}$$

V_{NTS} by pricing case, using Equation (11)

Cases	V_{NTS}
1, 2, 5, 9, 13, 14, 16	$\dfrac{\pi_X AT + (1-\pi_X) X_\mathrm{p}T}{1+r_z}$
3, 4, 6–8, 10–12, 15, 17, 18	$\dfrac{\pi_X AT + (1-\pi_X) AT}{1+r_z} = \dfrac{AT}{1+r_z}$
19, 20	$\dfrac{\pi_X X_\mathrm{o}T + (1-\pi_X) X_\mathrm{p}T}{1+r_z}$

$$\text{Cases} \qquad \beta_{NTS} = \frac{\Phi_{NTS,\mathrm{o}} - \Phi_{NTS,\mathrm{p}}}{V_{NTS}} \cdot \frac{\theta_X}{r_{\mathrm{e,o}} - r_{\mathrm{e,p}}} = \frac{\Phi_{NTS,\mathrm{o}} - \Phi_{NTS,\mathrm{p}}}{\pi_X \Phi_{NTS,\mathrm{o}} + (1-\pi_X)\Phi_{NTS,\mathrm{p}}} \cdot \frac{\theta_X(1+r_z)}{r_{\mathrm{e,o}} - r_{\mathrm{e,p}}}$$

β_{NTS} by pricing case, using Equation (12)

Cases	β_{NTS}
1, 2, 5, 9, 13, 14, 16	$\dfrac{AT - X_\mathrm{p}T}{\pi_X AT + (1-\pi_X) X_\mathrm{p}T} \cdot \dfrac{\theta_X(1+r_z)}{r_{\mathrm{e,o}} - r_{\mathrm{e,p}}} = \dfrac{A - X_\mathrm{p}}{\pi_X A + (1-\pi_X) X_\mathrm{p}} \cdot \dfrac{\theta_X(1+r_z)}{r_{\mathrm{e,o}} - r_{\mathrm{e,p}}}$
3, 4, 6–8, 10–12, 15, 17, 18	$\dfrac{AT - AT}{\pi_X AT + (1-\pi_X) AT} \cdot \dfrac{\theta_X(1+r_z)}{r_{\mathrm{e,o}} - r_{\mathrm{e,p}}} = 0$
19, 20	$\dfrac{X_\mathrm{o}T - X_\mathrm{p}T}{\pi_X X_\mathrm{o}T + (1-\pi_X) X_\mathrm{p}T} \cdot \dfrac{\theta_X(1+r_z)}{r_{\mathrm{e,o}} - r_{\mathrm{e,p}}} = \dfrac{X_\mathrm{o} - X_\mathrm{p}}{E^{\pi_X}(\tilde{X})} \cdot \dfrac{\theta_X \cdot (1+r_z)}{r_{\mathrm{e,o}} - r_{\mathrm{e,p}}} = \beta_X$

that solves:[16]

$$V_D = \frac{E_X^\pi(\tilde{\Phi}_D(r))}{1 + r_z} = D \tag{13}$$

for a proposed debt amount, D. Following this procedure, Table 5 derives the par yield for the 20 pricing cases in Table 3.

Step 3. Determine the Risks of the Tax Shields and the Claims

Once the par yield is determined, we can identify the risks of the tax shields and the other claims. Table 6 compares the magnitude of the debt tax shield risk to that of the unlevered firm and that of the debt. Table A.1 presents the returns betas of the tax shields, equity, tax claim and the firm $(D + E)$, and the marginal impact of debt on these betas.

Step 4. Determine Expected Rates of Return and Market Values

The approximate APT expression (5) links betas to expected rates of return. Substituting the returns betas from Table A.1 into Equation (5) yields the expected rates of return, or costs of capital.[17] The levered firm returns beta (β_{D+E}) and Equation (5) together yield the *WACC*. Knowing the expected cash flows and the cost of capital, the firm's value is implied by Equation (11). Table 7 contains the relevant expressions for the value of the levered firm.

---

[16]Merton's (1974) debt supply analysis ignores taxes. Miller's (1977) debt supply arguments emphasize personal taxes and general equilibrium—tax shield risk is not the focus.

[17]To express the cost of debt k_D in terms of fundamental parameters, eliminate r using the par yield expressions from Table 5.

Table 5. Debt pricing for the 2×2 model. The par yield is computed for each pricing case using the output apportionment formula for debt holders $\tilde{\Phi}_D$ (Table 2) and the *RNV* formula (11). The risk-neutral formula is inverted for the par yield r. Three distinct par yield expressions arise: r_D, r_{11}, and the riskless rate, r_z.

$$V_D = \frac{E^{\pi_X}(\tilde{\Phi}_D(r))}{1+r_z} = D$$

Cases	Par yield
Debt is risky, and firm pays taxes in states "o" and "p" (cases 1, 5, 6, 9, 10, 13, 16, 17, 19)	$\dfrac{\pi_X D(1+r) + (1-\pi_X)X_p}{1+r_z} = D$ $\qquad$ "r_D" $= \dfrac{r_z + (1-\pi_X)\left(\dfrac{D-X_p}{D}\right)}{\pi_X}$
Debt is risky, but no taxes are paid in state "p" (case 11)	$\dfrac{\pi_X D(1+r) + (1-\pi_X)(X_p(1-T)+(A+rD)T)}{1+r_z} = D$ $\quad$ "r_{11}" $= \dfrac{r_z + (1-\pi_X)\left(\dfrac{D-(X_p(1-T)+AT)}{D}\right)}{\pi_X + (1-\pi_X)T}$
Debt is riskless (cases 2–4, 7, 8, 12, 14, 15, 18, 20)	$\dfrac{\pi_X D(1+r) + (1-\pi_X)D(1+r)}{1+r_z} = D$ $\qquad$ r_z

Table 6. Relative magnitude of risks of the debt tax shield, the unlevered firm and the debt, for the 2×2 model with $\theta_X > 0$.

Description (cases)	β_{DTS} vs. β^U
Both DTS and D are risky (1, 2, 5, 9, 13–18)	$\beta_{DTS} > \beta^U$
Both DTS and D are risky (3, 6, 7, 10)	Sign varies
DTS riskless (4, 8, 11, 12)	$\beta_{DTS} = 0 < \beta^U$
DTS worthless (19, 20)	β_{DTS} is null

Description (cases)	β_{DTS} vs. β_D
Both DTS and D are risky (1–3, 5–7, 9, 10, 13–18)	$\beta_{DTS} > \beta_D$
Both DTS and D are riskless (4, 8, 12)	$\beta_{DTS} = \beta_D = 0$
DTS riskless; D risky (11)	$\beta_{DTS} = 0 < \beta_D$
DTS worthless (19, 20)	β_{DTS} is null

Table 7. Value of the levered firm and the marginal value impact of debt.

Cases	V_{D+E}	$\dfrac{\partial V_{D+E}}{\partial D}$
1, 5, 6, 9, 10	$\dfrac{\pi_X \left(X_o(1-T) + (A + Dr_D)T \right) + (1-\pi_X)X_p}{1 + r_z}$	$\dfrac{\pi_X r_D T}{1 + r_z} \cdot \dfrac{\partial r_D}{\partial D} > 0$
2, 3, 7	$\dfrac{\pi_X \left(X_o(1-T) + (A + Dr_z)T \right) + (1-\pi_X)X_p}{1 + r_z}$	$\dfrac{\pi_X r_z T}{1 + r_z} > 0$
4, 8, 12	$\dfrac{E^{\pi_X}(\tilde{X})(1-T) + (A + Dr_z)T}{1 + r_z}$	$\dfrac{r_z T}{1 + r_z} > 0$
11	$\dfrac{E^{\pi_X}(\tilde{X})(1-T) + (A + Dr_{11})T}{1 + r_z}$	$\dfrac{r_{11} T}{1 + r_z} \cdot \dfrac{\partial r_{11}}{\partial D} > 0$
13–20	$\dfrac{E^{\pi_X}(\tilde{X})}{1 + r_z}$	0

Chapter V

Discussion of Results

The Borrowing Rate Determines the Firm's Tax Obligations

The tax states depend, not surprisingly, on the magnitude of the borrowing rate. More interestingly, as Table 5 shows, three par yield expressions emerge (r_z, r_D, and r_{11}). When the debt is riskless the borrowing interest rate is $r = r_z$. With risky debt the par yield is increasing in D (Appendix A.2). This is because the bondholders face increasing default risk as leverage increases. Table 5 also shows that the magnitude of r, for a particular amount of risky debt, depends on whether or not the firm pays taxes in default. If the firm pays zero taxes in the default state, the par yield is r_D. If the firm pays taxes in default state the borrowing rate is r_{11} (case 11). This knowledge is important for at least two reasons. As will be seen, it permits an assessment of the risk of the tax shields, the after-tax cost of risky debt, and the value of the government's tax claim at any level of borrowing.

The Cost of Risky Debt

Consider the textbook question: What is the correct way to calculate the firm's after-tax cost of risky debt when the tax shields are risky? The answer to this question has remained unclear.[18]

In our framework, the after-tax cost of debt is k_D, the creditors' expected return on the debt, and not the after-tax par yield, $r(1-T)$, which is routinely used as a proxy for k_D.[19] This is because the par yield affects the debt's risk (note the dependence of β_D on r in Table A.1) and hence creditors' expected return, k_D. Intuitively, tax adjustments are already included in k_D, and no further tax adjustments are needed in determining the cost of debt. The economic cost of debt capital is the creditors' opportunity cost, and it depends on the expected return on alternative investments with the same risk. As long as their expected return is adequate, creditors do not care whether the firm can deduct interest payments for tax purposes.[20] No explicit tax adjustments are needed for estimating the cost of debt.

Risk of the Tax Shields and the Firm's Claims

As is well known, there is no consensus in the research about the tax shields' risks, and there is no clear answer about what discount

---

[18]The limitations of using the standard riskless debt formulation $r(1-T)$, where r is the borrowing rate and T is the firm's tax rate, are well known (see, e.g., Ross *et al.*, 1988, pp. 456–459; Grinblatt and Titman, 2002, p. 485). However, an alternative formulation consistent with the cost of capital theory has not been formally developed.

[19]The cost of debt capital formula takes on two different forms depending upon whether one thinks of the firm's accounting cost of debt capital or creditors' opportunity cost. The standard $1 - T$ tax adjustment is justified on the grounds that interest is tax deductible. If the argument is that a firm paying a riskless rate r has a tax shield of rT, then, in an accounting sense, the firm has incurred a net cash outflow of $r(1 - T)$ and this is the "book cost" of borrowing.

[20]Of course, tax effects are relevant to creditors. For example, in case 11 the tax rate appears in the par yield expression: In state "p" debt principal is only partially repaid, although the firm pays taxes. Thus, for a higher tax rate, less after-tax funds are available to repay creditors.

rate for the tax benefit of depreciation and interest is correct (e.g., Copeland *et al.*, 2000).[21] Our interest in this research is not on the tax shields' risks *per se*. Rather, the ability to model their risks analytically allows us to better understand how borrowing affects the firm's total risk (risk of debt plus equity). This knowledge is critical for correctly estimating the *WACC* and *MTR*. Identifying r endogenously allows us to specify the tax shields' risks correctly.

We find that the tax shields' risks depend on the magnitudes and characteristics of the firm's cash flows, its depreciable asset base, and financing details. Our findings are summarized in Table 6, which compares the risk of the debt tax shields with that of the unlevered firm and the risks of the debt tax shields with the risk of the debt.

Contrary to the routine assumption that the debt tax shield is as risky as the debt, we find that risky debt tax shields may be greater than, less than, or equal to the risk of both the debt and the unlevered firm. As seen in Table 6, the relative magnitudes of the debt tax shield risk versus the unlevered firm risk, and the risk of the debt relative to that of the debt tax shield risk are case specific. It is difficult to generalize. What we can say from Table 6, however, is that when both the debt and the interest tax shield are risky, the interest tax shield is riskier than the debt.

The risks of the firm's other claims (equity, debt, and the government's tax claim) are summarized in Table A.1. As can be seen,

---

[21]The common view that the debt shields are as risky as the interest payments (e.g., Myers, 1974; Taggart, 1991) is ad hoc. Miles and Ezzell (1980, 1985) assume that the risks of the firm's total assets, the unlevered assets, and the debt shields are about the same. Harris and Pringle (1985) argue that all tax shields should be discounted at the unlevered cost of equity, and Kaplan and Ruback (1995) discount the debt shield at the unlevered cost of equity. Luehrman (1997) maintains that tax shields should be discounted at a rate that lies between the cost of debt and the cost of unlevered equity. Also see Talmor *et al.* (1985), Green and Talmor (1985), and Ehrhardt and Daves (2002). In Ruback (2002), the risk of the interest tax shields matches that of the firm's assets. Fernandez (2004) assumes that the risk of the non-debt tax shields is the same as that of the unlevered firm and that the levered firm's tax shields have the same risk as the firm's equity.

the return betas for these claims depend on their tax treatment. The impact of borrowing on these claims is either zero, or it depends on the sign of θ_X. The sign of θ_X is positive (negative) when the firm's cash flows are positively (negatively) correlated with the exogenous economic shock. One would expect that for the typical firm, $\theta_X > 0$. Thus, borrowing will, for the typical firm, increase the risk of these claims.

The WACC

Since no explicit tax adjustments are required to compute k_D, one minus the tax rate does not appear in the *WACC* as a multiplicative coefficient on the debt coupon rate, as in the familiar expression:

$$WACC = \frac{D}{D + V_E} \cdot r\,(1 - T) + \frac{V_E}{D + V_E} \cdot k_E.$$

Instead, we have:

$$WACC = \frac{D}{D + V_E} \cdot k_D + \frac{V_E}{D + V_E} \cdot k_E,$$

with k_D, k_E, and V_E all non-linear functions of the tax rate. This, again, is because r is endogenous and is a function of the firm's tax shields. Tax effects are impounded into the market values and required rates of return on the debt and equity.[22]

The Marginal Effects of Borrowing on Firm Risk and the WACC

The prevailing view is that with corporate taxes (and no bankruptcy costs), increasing debt lowers firm risk (the risk of $D + E$, β_{D+E}). This belief rests on the assumption that the debt tax shield is riskless.

---

[22]The *WACC* can also be obtained by substituting the levered firm returns beta β_{D+E} from Table A.1 into Equation (5).

With risky debt and potentially redundant tax shields, we find that β_{D+E} and the *WACC* may fall, remain constant, or even rise with leverage increases, depending on the extent to which the firm can utilize the incremental deductions, which in turn affects the risk of the firm cash flow, $\tilde{\Phi}_{D+E}$.

Table A.1 shows if the total tax shield is riskless and $\theta_X > 0$, an extra dollar of borrowing lowers firm risk. To the extent that most firms' cash flows are positively correlated with the economy ($\theta_X > 0$), increasing debt lowers the risk of the firm, if the firm could utilize the incremental tax shield in all states. This is the case considered in the standard textbook result wherein debt lowers firm risk and hence the *WACC*. When the total tax shield is risky, the marginal impact of borrowing on firm risk is either zero or has the same sign as θ_X.[23] Thus, for a firm with $\theta_X > 0$, an extra dollar of borrowing may increase firm risk, if the incremental tax shield would not be fully utilized in all states.

The intuition for these results is provided in Figure 2, which depicts three scenarios that are obtained in regard to the incremental tax shields from borrowing. The kinked lines in these figures show the cash flow to $D + E$ for a given level of operating cash flows.

Consider first scenario 1, where $A + rD$ lies between the "up" and "down" state operating cash flows. When the firm increases borrowing by \$1 to a new level D', the interest rate on the debt rises from r to r'. This generates an incremental tax shield in state "o," and the firm's after-tax cash flow increases. The risks of the total tax shields and of the firm increase, but so does firm value.[24] In scenario 2, an

---

[23]In Table A.1, note that whenever cash flow is positive in state "o" and zero in state "p," the returns beta equals $\dfrac{1}{\pi_X} \cdot \dfrac{\theta_X \cdot (1 + r_z)}{r_{e,o} - r_{e,p}}$. It can be shown that if two claims have the same joint probability matrix with the priced risk factor and their cash flow distributions differ only by a multiplicative constant, then their returns betas are equal.

[24]Appendix A.5 helps explain why the returns betas of both the debt tax shield and the firm increase in this scenario.

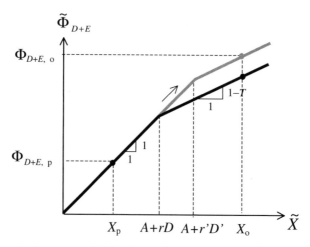

Scenario 1.   An incremental debt dollar (D increased to D' and par yield may increase, $r \leqslant r'$) generates incremental tax shield in state "o." If $\theta_X > 0$, β_{TTS} and β_{D+E} increase (see Table A.1 and Appendix A.5), but so do V_{TTS} and V_{D+E}. This situation arises in cases 1–3, 5–7, 9, and 10: $X_{\mathrm{p}} \leqslant A + rD < X_{\mathrm{o}}$.

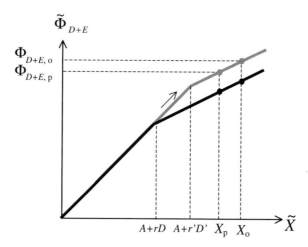

Scenario 2.   An incremental debt dollar generates incremental debt tax shield in both states. If $\theta_X > 0$, β_{D+E} falls and V_{D+E} rises. This situation arises in cases 4, 8, 11, and 12: $A + rD < X_{\mathrm{p}}$.

Figure 2. Impact of an incremental debt dollar on levered firm risk and value.

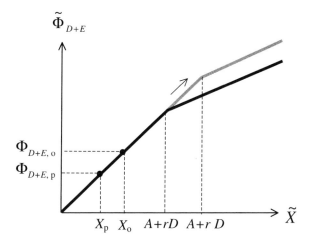

Scenario 3. An incremental debt dollar produces no incremental tax shield. β_{D+E} and V_{D+E} are unaffected. This situation arises in cases 13–20: $X_o \leqslant A + rD$.

Figure 2. (*Continued*)

incremental debt dollar generates tax shields in both the "o" and the "p" states, causing levered firm cash flows to increase by an equal amount.

This reduces the returns beta and increases firm value. In scenario 3 the debt increase does not affect firm risk. The incremental borrowing yields no tax benefit, since the incremental tax shield from the debt increase is unused in both states of nature. Since firm cash flow is unaltered, β_{D+E} is unchanged.

The Marginal Effects of Debt on Firm Value

MM (1963) showed that with riskless debt and tax benefits (and no bankruptcy costs) the firm maximizes debt. Our framework allows us to examine how this result changes with risky debt and risky tax shields. This question is particularly interesting because as just seen, the firm's risk and its *WACC* can, in fact, increase with borrowing. As it turns out, and somewhat surprisingly, we find that the firm will still optimally maximize debt, and that the MM all-debt result is preserved.[25]

To see why, revisit Figure 2 and consider a firm with $\theta_X > 0$. As noted in the figure, the risk of the tax shields and of the firm increases with the marginal debt dollar in scenario 1, but firm value also increases because the firm's cash flows increase proportionately more than enough to compensate for the increase in risk. In scenario 2, debt lowers firm risk and hence increases firm value. In scenario 3, borrowing does not affect the tax shields' risk or firm value. Scenario 3 corresponds, however, to a firm with uneconomic investments ($NPV_A < 0$, cases 13–20).

Thus, a viable firm optimally borrows up to debt capacity, even when its cost of capital is increasing in the amount borrowed. This result is obtained because the increase in the firm's expected cash flow arising from the marginal tax shields outweighs the effects of any increase in the $WACC$.

Debt Capacity

MM (1963) showed that the firm can borrow "up to firm value." Their argument, however, is a legal implication of equity's limited liability (equity cannot have a negative value) and, since it says little about the debt level or firm value at which this upper bound is reached, it is not an economic explanation for the borrowing limit. (Also see Myers, 1977.)

Our model identifies the firm's debt capacity (Appendix A.3)— the debt level at which it can borrow no more. Debt capacity, $D_{\max}$, is the highest level of D for which the debt can be fairly priced at par and at which the *ex dividend* equity value approaches zero from above. The par yield, as noted, is increasing in D for risky debt (Appendix A.2); however, r can only be computed up to a certain

---

[25]Internal optimal capital structures with corporate taxes were obtained in Brennan and Schwartz (1978) and Turnbull (1979) because the borrowing interest rate is held fixed for all borrowing levels and because of bankruptcy costs.

debt amount. Although r increases with D, creditors' expected rate of return eventually falls short of their required rate of return, irrespective of r. Beyond this point, the debt cannot be rationally priced, the supply of additional credit evaporates, and the firm reaches debt capacity. It cannot borrow any more, irrespective of how high a coupon rate that it is prepared to offer.

Our result is consistent (as it should be) with limited liability, but our credit supply side route to debt capacity links the borrowing limit to characteristics of the output distribution and exogenous economic variables. The characteristics of the investment and exogenous economic (the riskless rate and the market risk premium) and policy variables (the riskless rate, the statutory tax rate, the cash flow distribution, and the risk-neutral probabilities that depend on the economic variables, Appendix A.3) together determine this upper limit to borrowing.[26]

If the firm's investment is viable on a pre-tax basis ($NPV_A > 0$) then at debt capacity the firm is tax-paying and $D > A$ (Appendix A.3 and A.4). In this case, just as in MM, the firm borrows more than the value of the physical assets generating the cash flows. However, if $NPV_A \leq 0$ the firm can borrow no more than the value of its cash flows. An implication is that we may be able to better understand firms' borrowing decisions by shifting our focus away from the right- and onto the left-hand side (the assets side) of the firm's economic balance sheet.

The "Three Claims View" of the Firm

The standard theory views the firm as consisting of two claims on the output—the equity and the debt. The tax authority is also a

---

[26]It is often assumed (e.g., Myers, 1974) that the firm's limit to debt usage is exogenously given. Turnbull (1979, p. 938) argues that the adjusted present value criterion rests on ad hoc assumptions about the functional form of the debt capacity constraint.

claimant on output (Miller, 1988), but this intuition has not been formalized with risky debt [Galai (1998) assumes riskless debt].

Our model *de facto* treats the government as a third claimant. Firm value is the same irrespective of whether it is assumed that after-tax output is distributed between two claims (debt and equity), or whether the pre-tax output is assumed to be apportioned among three claims (equity, debt, and tax): $V_E + V_D = (1 - T) \cdot V_X + V_{NTS} + V_{DTS} = V_X - V_T$.

The advantage of the "three-claims" view of the firm is that it lends itself to numerical illustration, and hence to the endogenous determination of the *MTR*. Moreover, it permits analysis of the wealth implications of alternative tax and interest rate policy decisions. The sensitivity of interest rate and tax policy changes on firms' economic balance sheets, and hence inventors' wealth can, in principle, be evaluated in our model.[27] Appendix B illustrates how our framework can be used to identify, numerically, how firms' balance sheets change across all feasible borrowing levels given exogenous economic variables such as the corporate tax rate and the riskless interest rate.

The Value of the Tax Claim

The literature routinely assumes that the firm can borrow until it altogether eliminates its tax liability. However, this is inconsistent with the evidence that corporations do not use debt up to the point that tax shields are maximized (Graham, 2000). This is often interpreted to mean that managers are "leaving money on the table."

Our model provides an explanation for this empirical finding. We find that for a positive NPV_A firm at debt capacity, the value of the tax claim is positive (Appendix A.4). That is, with rationally

---

[27]Various authors (e.g., Majd and Myers, 1985) have noted that, to evaluate the implications of taxes and tax policy changes, one needs a theory that can link these policy changes to the economic (market) values of the various claims.

priced debt, the firm cannot fully eliminate its tax obligation by issuing additional debt. The intuition is straightforward. As a residual claim, equity cannot have zero value in a viable firm. The firm must therefore have taxable income in at least one state, in which case, the current value of the tax claim must also be positive. Otherwise, the debt cannot be rationally priced.

Effective *MTR*

The firm's *MTR* is an implication of modeling the firm's borrowing. It is a numerical result that is inferred after the coupon rate, the risks, and values of the claims have been identified. For this reason, we will discuss the *MTR* later, in the context of our numerical examples.

Chapter VI

Extension to $s \times s$ States

The probability matrix (9) can be expanded to $s \times s$ states $(s > 2)$. Consider a joint probability matrix $\underset{s \times s}{\mathbf{P}}$ containing elements $\mathrm{p}_{i,j}$:

$$
\begin{array}{c|cccc|c}
 & r_{e,1} & r_{e,2} & \cdots & r_{e,s} & \\
\hline
\Phi_1 & \mathrm{p}_{11} & \mathrm{p}_{12} & \cdots & \mathrm{p}_{1s} & \mathrm{P}_1 \\
\Phi_2 & \mathrm{p}_{21} & \mathrm{p}_{22} & \cdots & \mathrm{p}_{2s} & \mathrm{P}_2 \\
\vdots & \vdots & \vdots & \ddots & \vdots & \vdots \\
\Phi_s & \mathrm{p}_{s1} & \mathrm{p}_{s2} & \cdots & \mathrm{p}_{ss} & \mathrm{P}_s \\
\hline
 & \mathrm{P}_{e,1} & \mathrm{P}_{e,2} & \cdots & \mathrm{P}_{e,s} &
\end{array}
\quad , \tag{14}
$$

where $\underset{s \times 1}{\boldsymbol{\Phi}} = [\Phi_1 \, \Phi_2 \cdots \Phi_s]'$ are the state cash flows and $\underset{s \times 1}{\mathbf{r}} = [r_{e,1} \, r_{e,2} \cdots r_{e,s}]'$ are the state returns on the priced risk factor. Using the identity vector $\underset{s \times 1}{\mathbf{i}} = [1 \, 1 \cdots 1]'$, the state probabilities of the priced risk factor are $[\mathrm{P}_{e,1} \, \mathrm{P}_{e,2} \cdots \mathrm{P}_{e,s}]' = \mathbf{i}' \, \mathbf{P}$, and the state cash flow probabilities are $[\mathrm{P}_1 \, \mathrm{P}_2 \cdots \mathrm{P}_s] = (\mathbf{Pi})'$. With single-factor pricing, the certainty-equivalent valuation expression [the $s \times s$-state analog to Equation (8)] is:

$$V_{\boldsymbol{\Phi}} = \frac{\mathbf{i}'\mathbf{P}'\boldsymbol{\Phi} - \dfrac{\mathbf{i}\left[\mathbf{P}*\left[\boldsymbol{\Phi} - \mathbf{i}'\mathbf{P}'\boldsymbol{\Phi}\mathbf{i}\right]\left[\mathbf{r} - \mathbf{i}'\mathbf{Pri}\right]'\right]\mathbf{i}'}{\left[\mathbf{i}'\mathbf{P}\right]\left[\left[\mathbf{r} - \mathbf{i}'\mathbf{Pri}\right]*\left[\mathbf{r} - \mathbf{i}'\mathbf{Pri}\right]\right]}\left[\mathbf{i}'\mathbf{Pr} - r_z\right]}{1 + r_z},$$

where "*" denotes element-wise multiplication (Hadamard product). Collecting terms in $\boldsymbol{\Phi}$ yields the *RNV* expression [the $s \times s$ analog to Equation (11)]:

$$V_{\boldsymbol{\Phi}} = \frac{\boldsymbol{\pi}'_{\boldsymbol{\Phi}}\boldsymbol{\Phi}}{1 + r_z}, \quad \text{where}$$

$$\underset{s\times 1}{\boldsymbol{\pi}_{\boldsymbol{\Phi}}} = \mathbf{Pi} - \frac{\left[\mathbf{P} - (\mathbf{Pi})(\mathbf{i}'\mathbf{P})\right]\left[\mathbf{r} - \mathbf{i}'\mathbf{Pri}\right]}{\left[\mathbf{i}'\mathbf{P}\right]\left[\left[\mathbf{r} - \mathbf{i}'\mathbf{Pri}\right]*\left[\mathbf{r} - \mathbf{i}'\mathbf{Pri}\right]\right]}\left[\mathbf{i}'\mathbf{Pr} - r_z\right]. \qquad (15)$$

The term $\boldsymbol{\pi}_{\boldsymbol{\Phi}}$ is equal to the state cash flow probability vector minus a vector of risk adjustments.

Using $\boldsymbol{\pi}_{\boldsymbol{\Phi}}$, the par yield is computed for a given D by iterating the $s \times s$-state analog of Equation (13) on r until the expression holds with equality; debt capacity is computed by iterating on D and r simultaneously until the $s \times s$-state analog of Equation (13) holds with equality and the equity cash flow approaches zero from above. Once r is computed, the remaining claims are valued using Equation (15). Returns betas are computed using $s \times s$-state analogs of Equations (5)–(8).

Chapter VII

Numerical Illustration

This chapter illustrates the model numerically and graphically. Table 8 lists the parameter values assumed for the 2×2 and 5×5 examples.[28] The initial investment of $A = \$100,000$ produces an uncertain $\tilde{X}$ with expected value \$135,000. The corporate tax rate is $T = 30\%$, and the riskless rate is $r_z = 8\%$. For the 5×5 example the elements of the $\tilde{X}$ and $\tilde{r}_e$ vectors and the 5×5 probability matrix are chosen such that $E(\tilde{X}), E(\tilde{r}_e), VAR(\tilde{X}), VAR(\tilde{r}_e)$, and $COV(\tilde{X}, \tilde{r}_e)$ closely match the corresponding values in the 2×2 example.

Given this information, Figure 3 shows how the coupon rate changes with debt. The debt becomes risky in the 2×2 example at $D = \$46,296.30$, and in the 5×5 example the debt is risky at borrowing amounts above \$76,719.29. Note that the standard definition of the after-tax cost of debt, $r(1 - T)$ (borrowing rate multiplied by one minus the tax rate), yields a generally biased proxy for k_D.

---

[28]Additional computed values are shown in Tables B.1 and B.2.

Table 8. Numerical illustration: parameters assumed.

Joint distribution of output $\tilde{X}$ and the priced risk factor $\tilde{r}_e$:

2 × 2 example

	$r_{e,o} = 0.15$	$r_{e,p} = -0.05$		Risk-neutral probs, by Equation (11)
		$p_{op} = 0.05$	$P_o = 0.85$	$\pi_X = 0.7284$
$X_o = 150.000$	$p_{oo} = 0.80$	$p_{pp} = 0.1$	$X_o = 0.15$	$1 - \pi_X = 0.1716$
$X_p = 50.000$	$p_{po} = 0.05$	$P_{e,p} = 0.15$		
	$P_{e,o} = 0.85$			

5 × 5 example

	$r_{e,1} = 0.2196$	$r_{e,2} = 0.1600$	$r_{e,3} = 0.12$	$r_{e,4} = 0.080$	$r_{e,5} = 0.0206$		Risk-neutral probs, by Equation (15)
$X_1 = 187,146.40$	$p_{11} = 0.1815$	$p_{12} = 0$	$p_{13} = 0$	$p_{14} = 0$	$p_{15} = 0.0463$	$P_1 = 0.2278$	$\pi_1 = 0.12213$
$X_2 = 145,005.02$	$p_{21} = 0$	$p_{22} = 0.1815$	$p_{23} = 0$	$p_{24} = 0$	$p_{25} = 0$	$P_2 = 0.1815$	$\pi_2 = 0.12450$
$X_3 = 135,000.00$	$p_{31} = 0$	$p_{32} = 0$	$p_{33} = 0.1815$	$p_{34} = 0$	$p_{35} = 0$	$P_3 = 0.1815$	$\pi_3 = 0.18149$
$X_4 = 124,994.98$	$p_{41} = 0$	$p_{42} = 0$	$p_{43} = 0$	$p_{44} = 0.1815$	$p_{45} = 0$	$P_4 = 0.1815$	$\pi_4 = 0.23849$
$X_5 = 82,853.60$	$p_{51} = 0.0463$	$p_{52} = 0$	$p_{53} = 0$	$p_{54} = 0$	$p_{55} = 0.1815$	$P_5 = 0.2278$	$\pi_5 = 0.33339$
	$P_{e,1} = 0.2278$	$P_{e,2} = 0.1815$	$P_{e,3} = 0.1815$	$P_{e,4} = 0.1815$	$P_{e,5} = 0.2278$		

(*Continued*)

Table 8. (*Continued*)

Initial investment, A	100,000
Corporate tax rate, T	0.3
Expected return on a zero-beta asset, r	0.08

Computed values:	2×2 example	5×5 example
Expected output, $E(\tilde{X})$	135,000	135,000.00
Expected return on the priced risk factor, $E(\tilde{r}_e)$	0.12	0.1200
Variance of output, $VAR(\tilde{X})$	1.275E + 9	1.275E + 9
Variance of the return on the priced risk factor, $VAR(\tilde{r}_e)$	0.0051	0.0051
Covariance of output with the priced risk factor, $COV(\tilde{X}, \tilde{r}_e)$	1.55E + 3	1.55E + 3
Correlation of output with the priced risk factor, $CORR(\tilde{X}, \tilde{r}_e)$	0.6078	0.6078
Risk-adjustment term, θ_X, by Equation (10)	0.6078	–
Expected output under the risk-neutral probabilities, $E^{\pi}X(\tilde{X})$	122,843.14	122,843.20
Cash flow beta of output, $\mathbf{B}_X$, by Equation (10)	3.039E + 5	3.039E + 5
Returns beta of output, β_X, by Equation (12)	2.672	2.672
Required rate of return on output, k_X	0.1869	0.1869
Value of output, V_X, by Equation (11)	113,743.65	113,743.71
Pre-tax net present value of investment plan, NPV_A, by Equation (1)	13,743.65	13,743.71

2 x 2 example

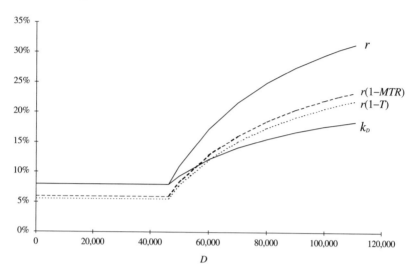

5 x 5 example

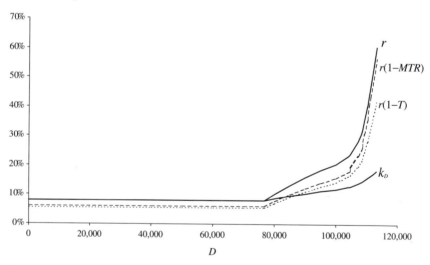

Figure 3.   Par yield (r) and the cost of debt (k_D) for the numerical examples (data from Table 8 and Appendix B). When the debt is riskless, the par yield and the cost of debt are equal. For risky debt, $r > k_D$. Two proxies for k_D are also shown for comparison: the par yield times one minus the tax rate (the dotted line) and the par yield times one minus the expected MTR.

$r(1 - MTR)$ is closer to k_D than $r(1 - T)$ for low debt levels but is a worse proxy for high debt levels. Even with riskless debt, $r(1 - T) \neq k_D$, and as D is increased $r(1 - T)$ first understates and then overstates k_D.

Figure 4 shows how the risk of the tax shields change with debt. The risk of the depreciation tax shield β_{NTS} is fixed, due to our assumption about the seniority of depreciation over interest deductions. The risk of the debt tax shield is relatively insensitive to borrowing at low debt levels but rises dramatically at high debt levels.

Figure 5 plots the costs of debt and equity and the *WACC* for different debt amounts. In the 5×5 example, the *WACC* increases with debt from 16.56% to 18.22%. The cost of debt does not increase much because as debt increases, the value of the tax shields also increases, thus providing additional protection for the debt. The *WACC* does not increase much, because as debt increases, although the cost of equity increases rapidly, its contribution to the *WACC* is dampened by the fact that the value of the equity as a proportion of total capitalization falls rapidly. The *WACC*, except at very low levels of debt, can be significantly affected by how one defines the firm's cost of debt.[29] These results have potentially important implications for low and highly-levered firms. Figure 6 shows that in highly leveraged firms, the *WACC* in our model is significantly lower than that implied by using either $r(1 - T)$ (the standard textbook k_D proxy) or $r(1 - MTR)$, which is commonly used in the industry as a proxy for k_D.

The formulas for computing debt capacity are presented in Appendix A.3. Debt capacity is \$110,661.75 for the 2×2 example and is \$113,108.40 in the 5×5 example. The value of the tax claim is positive, even at debt capacity.[30] Figure 7 and Table A.2 show the

---

[29] Although not apparent in Figure 5, the *WACC* increases for the 5×5 example from 16.56% (at $D = 0$) to 18.22% at debt capacity ($D = \$113,108.41$).
[30] At debt capacity the tax claim is worth \$3,082 and \$635 (for the 2×2 and 5×5 examples, respectively).

2 x 2 example

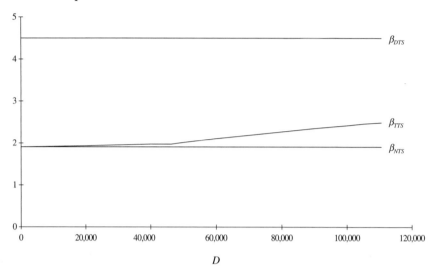

5 x 5 example

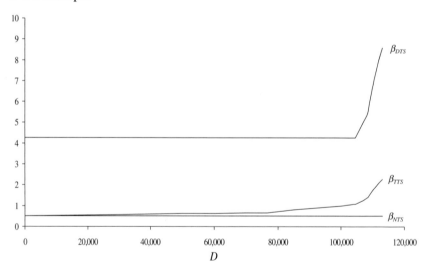

Figure 4.   Risk of the tax shields for the numerical examples (data from Appendix B). β_{NTS} = depreciation tax shield, β_{DTS} = debt tax shield, and β_{TTS} = total tax shield.

2 x 2 example

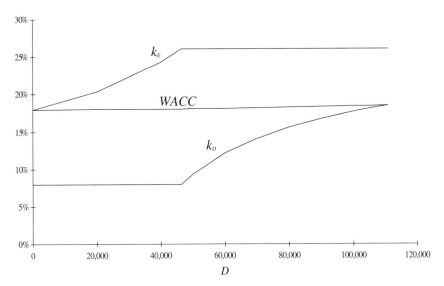

5 x 5 example

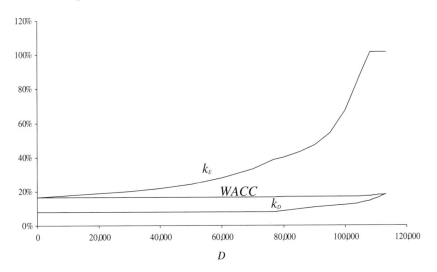

Figure 5. Cost of equity, k_E, cost of debt, k_D, and the $WACC$ for the numerical examples (data from Appendix B).

2 x 2 example

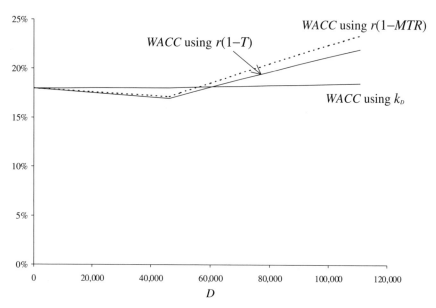

5 x 5 example

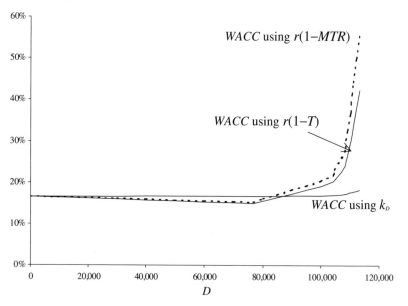

Figure 6.   WACC from the numerical examples, and WACC computed using $r(1-T), r(1-MTR)$ as proxies for k_D (data from Table A.2 and Appendix B).

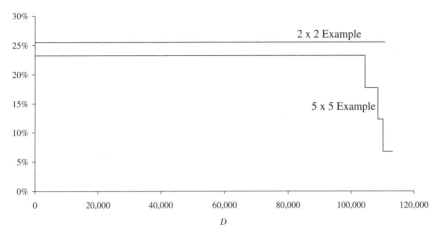

Figure 7.   Expected post-financing *MTR*s for the numerical examples. Data from Table 8 and Table A.2.

expected post-financing *MTR* for various debt amounts. The *MTR* is computed (using the state probabilities in Table 8) as the sum of the products of applicable tax rates (tax payment divided by taxable income) in each state of nature, times the state probabilities. In the 2×2 example, since taxable income is negative in state "p" for any debt amount, the applicable tax rate in that state is zero, hence the marginal expected tax rate is less than the statutory tax rate of 30%. Multiplying the relevant binomial probabilities ($P_o = 0.85$ and $P_o = 0.15$ from Table 8) and summing yield the 25.5% marginal expected tax rate. In the 5×5 example, for low debt levels taxes are paid in all states except one; as debt is increased, taxes paid fall to zero in additional states, causing the *MTR* to drop from 23% to 7%.[31]

---

[31]Graham (1996a) computes the expected *MTR* as the present value of taxes paid on an incremental dollar of taxable income using multi-period Monte Carlo simulation, an increasing tax rate schedule, tax loss carry forwards, investment tax credits, and the alternative minimum tax. Since ours is a one-period model, for simplicity we do not discount the tax payment when computing the expected marginal tax rate, though we could have, since we have the proper discount rate, k_T.

Ibbotson Associates, in its *Cost of Capital Yearbook*, provides cost of capital estimates using MTR estimates generated using Graham's (1996a) Monte Carlo methodology. Graham does not model the discount rate for valuing the tax shields, and he discounts tax payments using the average corporate debt yield. In our 5×5 example, we find that the discount rate for the tax claim exceeds the coupon rate[32]; the industry approach may thus be underestimating the true discount rate for the tax payments.

---

[32]In Appendix B, in the 5×5 example we have $k_T > r$ for all debt levels.

Chapter VIII

Conclusion

How firms estimate their $WACC$ and MTR is no trivial matter. A few percent in capital costs can mean a swing in billions of expenditure dollars (Bruner *et al.*, 1998). For this reason, US policy makers evaluate alternative tax policies by studying how they can influence, through the $WACC$ and MTR, firms' investment decisions.[33]

In this research, we have developed a cost of capital theory with risky debt and corporate taxes. Our methodology integrates the

---

[33]Congressional tax policy analysis presumes that the average corporate tax liability and the present value of tax depreciation are two of four critical factors affecting investment ["Joint Committee on Taxation, Overview of Work of the Staff of the Joint Committee on Taxation to Model the Macroeconomic Effects of Proposed Tax Legislation to Comply with House Rules XIII.3.(h)(2)(JCX-105-03)," US Congress, 2003]. Consistent with this, the evidence reviewed in Caballero (1999) corroborates the long-term link between investment and cost of capital. In a different context, Rosen (1998) argues that the cost of capital affects entrepreneurs' investment decisions. Also see Auerbach (1983) and Auerbach and Hassett (1992). Reinschmidt (2002) discusses how the cost of capital is used for public sector project analysis.

state pricing and beta pricing frameworks in a single-period approximate APT model, and captures interactions between the $WACC$ and the MTR. With this integration, the value of any claim (equity, debt, and tax) on the firm is invariant to the valuation methodology employed—it is the same using either the martingale (state pricing) or the risk-adjusted discount rate (beta pricing) approach. The net result of this integration is an internally consistent $WACC$ with corporate taxes, risky debt, and possibly redundant tax shields.

The model yields a "fully specified" cost of capital theory in the sense that, given details of the firm's investment plan and exogenous economic variables, it identifies, numerically, the marginal effects of debt for any feasible borrowing level. Specifically, the model (i) generates the firm's borrowing schedule—the borrowing rate (r, coupon rate) as a function of debt, (ii) identifies debt capacity (the maximum feasible borrowing) in terms of the firm's investment characteristics, (iii) identifies the risks, expected rates of return, and values of the tax shields and of the debt, the equity, and the government's claims, (iv) shows how the $WACC$ changes with borrowing, and (v) yields the expected post-financing MTR.

When the debt is risky and the firm has potentially redundant tax shields, generalizations about tax shields' risks are difficult. Precise statements require knowledge of the magnitudes of the various firm-specific and economy-wide parameters, and a case-by-case analysis is required. Nevertheless, several interesting and useful results are obtained.

The firm's after-tax cost of debt is the creditors' opportunity cost. This is not surprising but, more interestingly, we have shown that the creditors' opportunity cost already impounds the implications of tax effects; no further tax adjustment is necessary. We have also shown that the standard textbook definition of the after-tax cost of debt (r multiplied by one minus the tax rate) and the formula used in industry (r multiplied by one minus the MTR) are both biased estimates of the cost of debt.

Tax effects are, through the cost of debt, also impounded into our *WACC* formula; again, no multiplicative tax adjustment (one minus the tax rate) is necessary. We find that in high-debt firms the *WACC* is significantly lower than that implied using both the textbook and the industry proxies for the cost of debt. In our numerical examples, the latter formulation is closer to the true cost of debt than the textbook definition for low debt levels, but is a worse proxy for high debt levels. These results have potentially important implications for valuation and other analyses of low and highly-levered firms.

Graham (1996a) uses Monte Carlo methodology to estimate firms' *MTR*s.[34] His empirical methodology discounts the tax payment using the average corporate debt yield. We determine the correct discount rate for tax payments, and find that this rate exceeds the coupon rate for all debt amounts. Ibbotson Associates provides cost of capital estimates (these are reported in their *Cost of Capital Yearbook*) using *MTR* estimates generated with the Graham methodology, and our findings suggest that these industry estimates may underestimate the true discount rate.

Contrary to the riskless debt case wherein the firm's risk and *WACC* decrease with leverage, we have shown that with risky debt the *WACC* may increase, decrease, or remain constant. Which of these situations are obtained depends on the relevant magnitudes in the analysis, and the extent to which the tax shields are usable in each state. We have provided graphical intuition for these results.

Our analysis shows that the firm's debt capacity is determined by characteristics of its investment and exogenous economic variables. Specifically, the cash flow distribution, exogenous economic factors (riskless rate and the market risk premium and the risk-neutral probabilities that depend on the economic variables) and policy variables

---

[34]Graham's methodology accommodates multi-period tax code features (an increasing tax rate schedule, tax loss carry forwards, investment tax credits, and the alternative minimum tax) but he does not model the discount rate for the tax shields.

(the riskless rate, the statutory tax rate, Appendix A.3) together determine debt capacity. An implication is that we may be able to better understand firms' capital structure decisions by shifting our focus onto the left-hand side (the assets side) of firms' economic balance sheets.

We find, surprisingly, that even with risky debt and possibly redundant tax shields, the firm optimally maximizes leverage, and the MM "all debt" result is sustained. The firm optimally borrows up to debt capacity, even when its cost of capital is increasing in the amount borrowed. This result holds with risky debt because the increase in the firm's expected cash flow arising from the marginal tax shields outweighs the effects of any increase in the *WACC*.

The marginal effects of borrowing depend on the firm's investment characteristics, exogenous economic factors, and tax and interest rate details. A distinctive feature of our model is that it shows, numerically, how each debt dollar affects the entire economic balance sheet. The model shows how leverage alters not just the value of the debt and equity, but also the government's tax claim. It thus provides a potentially useful tool for examining the relation between interest rate and tax policy changes and resultant changes in firms' economic balance sheets.[35]

The need to extend the model analytically to a multi-period setting and to admit dynamic features of the tax code is clear. However,

---

[35] Alan Greenspan has recently articulated the need for this: "... Our analytic tools are going to have to increasingly focus on changes in asset values and resulting balance sheet variations if we are to understand these important economic forces. Central bankers, in particular, are going to have to be able to ascertain how changes in the balance sheets of economic actors influence real economic activity, and hence affect appropriate macroeconomic policies." (*New Challenges for Monetary Policy*, FRB of Kansas City Symposium, Jackson Hole, August 27, 1999). Also see Scholes and Wolfson (1992) for a discussion of how tax and interest rate polices can have far-reaching implications for pension planning, the evolution of alternative organizational forms, compensation structures in the economy, retirement planning, and business reorganizations.

this is a formidable task. The researcher attempting this generalization must model the firm's borrowing interest rate in a multi-period world wherein the coupon rate will be determined endogenously by dynamic features of the tax code. The single-period APT is inadequate; a multi-period formulation will be required. Nevertheless, subsequent refinements and extensions of this model (with, perhaps, Monte Carlo methods) to a multi-period setting can enrich the framework to accommodate tax loss carry forwards, personal taxes, tax credits, and bankruptcy costs, and offers the potential for a better understanding of the firm's financing and investment decisions.

Appendix A

Discussion of Various Results

A.1 Sign of NPV_A

Consider the pricing cases in Table 3. For cases 1–8, the sign of NPV_A may vary. Cases 9–12 involve $A < D$, and since $D \leqslant V_X$ we have $A < V_X$; hence $NPV_A > 0$ by Equation (1). In cases 14, 15, and 18, $D \leqslant A$ and $X_o \leqslant Dr_z + A$. Now $X_p \leqslant X_o$

$$\Rightarrow (1 - \pi_X) X_p \leqslant (1 - \pi_X) X_o \Rightarrow \pi_X X_o + (1 - \pi_X) X_p \leqslant X_o$$
$$\Rightarrow E^{\pi_X}(\tilde{X}) \leqslant Dr_z + A \leqslant Ar_z + A$$
$$\Rightarrow V_X \leqslant \frac{Ar_z + A}{1 + r_z} = A \Rightarrow NPV_A \leqslant 0.$$

In cases 13, 16, and 17, $D \leqslant A$ and $X_o \leqslant Dr_D + A$. Substituting for r_D,

$$X_o \leqslant \frac{D}{\pi_X}\left(r_z + (1 - \pi_X)\left(\frac{D - X_p}{D}\right)\right) + A.$$

Multiplying by π_X and adding $(1 - \pi_X)X_{\mathrm{p}}$,

$$\pi_X X_{\mathrm{o}} + (1 - \pi_X)X_{\mathrm{p}} \leqslant D(1 + r_z - \pi_X) + \pi_X A$$

$$\Rightarrow V_X \leqslant D + \left(\frac{\pi_X}{1 + r_z}\right)(A - D)$$

$$\Rightarrow V_X \leqslant \frac{\pi_X}{1 + r_z}A + \left(1 - \frac{\pi_X}{1 + r_z}\right)D \leqslant A \Rightarrow NPV_A \leqslant 0.$$

In cases 19 and 20, $X_{\mathrm{o}} < A$. Since $X_{\mathrm{p}} \leqslant X_{\mathrm{o}}$ and $\pi_X \leqslant 1$,

$$E^{\pi_X}(\tilde{X}) \leqslant X_0 \Rightarrow \frac{E^{\pi_X}(\tilde{X})}{1 + r_z} \leqslant X_{\mathrm{o}} < A \Rightarrow V_X < A \Rightarrow NPV_A \leqslant 0.$$

A.2 The Par Yield is Non-Decreasing in D

From the par yield expressions (Table 5),

$$\mathrm{sign}\left\{\frac{\partial r_D}{\partial D}\right\} = \mathrm{sign}\left\{\frac{1 - \pi_X}{\pi_X} \cdot X_{\mathrm{p}}\right\} > 0,$$

$$\mathrm{sign}\left\{\frac{\partial r_{11}}{\partial D}\right\} = \mathrm{sign}\left\{\frac{1 - \pi_X}{\pi_X + (1 - \pi_X)T} \cdot (X_{\mathrm{p}}(1 - T) + AT)\right\} > 0,$$

and

$$\frac{\partial r_Z}{\partial D} = 0.$$

That is, the par yield is increasing in D when the debt is risky; with riskless debt, the par yield is constant.

A.3 Debt Capacity

D can be increased until $X^* = X_{\mathrm{o}}$. At that point, state "o" output is just sufficient to fully repay creditors, and the cash flow to equity approaches zero from above. D cannot be increased further, since the equity cash flow would then be zero in both states, making creditors owners *ex ante*. From Table 3, $X^* = X_{\mathrm{o}}$ can occur only in cases 9–12 for an $NPV_A > 0$ firm or in cases 16–20 for an $NPV_A \leqslant 0$ firm. We consider these nine cases, and utilize the results that X^* is increasing in D and $A < D \Rightarrow Dr + A < X^*$ (note that $X^* = \frac{D(1+r(1-T))-AT}{1-T} = D(1+r) + \frac{T(D-A)}{1-T} > Dr + D > Dr + A$).

For cases 9 and 10, at debt capacity we have $X_p < Dr_D + A < X^* = X_o$. Now

$$\frac{D_{MAX,9-10}\left(1 + r_{D_{MAX,9-10}}(1-T)\right) - AT}{1-T} = X_o$$

$$\Rightarrow r_{D_{MAX,9-10}} = \frac{X_o(1-T) + AT - D_{MAX,9-10}}{D_{MAX,9-10}(1-T)}.$$

The debt is priced as

$$D_{MAX,9-10} = \frac{\pi_X D_{MAX,9-10}\left(1 + r_{D_{MAX,9-10}}\right) + (1 - \pi_X)X_p}{1 + r_z},$$

and substituting for $r_{D_{MAX,9-10}}$,

$$D_{MAX,9-10} = \frac{E^{\pi_X}(\tilde{X}) + \frac{\pi_X AT}{1-T}}{1 + r_z + \frac{\pi_X T}{1-T}}.$$

In case 11, at debt capacity we have $X_p < Dr_{11} + A < X^* = X_o$.

$$X^* = \frac{D_{MAX,11}\left(1 + r_{D_{MAX,11}}(1-T)\right) - AT}{1-T} = X_o$$

$$\Rightarrow r_{D_{MAX,11}} = \frac{X_o(1-T) + AT - D_{MAX,11}}{D_{MAX,11}(1-T)}.$$

The debt is priced as

$$D_{MAX,11} =$$
$$\frac{\pi_X D_{MAX,11}\left(1 + r_{D_{MAX,11}}\right) + (1 - \pi_X)\left(X_p(1-T) + \left(A + D_{MAX,11} r_{D_{MAX,11}}\right)T\right)}{1 + r_z},$$

and substituting for $r_{D_{MAX,11}}$,

$$D_{MAX,11} = \frac{E^{\pi_X}(\tilde{X}) + \frac{AT}{1-T} + (1 - \pi_X)(X_o - X_p)T}{1 + r_z + \frac{T}{1-T}}.$$

In case 12, $X^* \leqslant X_p$, and D can be increased until cases 9, 10, or 11 is obtained. In cases 16 and 17, $X_p < D(1 + r_D) = X_o$, and the debt is priced as

$$D_{MAX,16-17} = \frac{\pi_X D_{MAX,16-17}(1+r_D) + (1-\pi_X)X_p}{1+r_z}$$

$$= \frac{\pi_X X_o + (1-\pi_X)X_p}{1+r_z} = V_X.$$

In case 18, $D(1+r_z) \leqslant X_p \leqslant X_o \leqslant A + r_z D$, and D can be increased until case 16 or 17 is obtained. Case 19 involves $X_p < D(1+r_D) \leqslant X_o$. When $X_p < D(1+r_D) = X_o$, the debt is priced as

$$D_{MAX,19} = \frac{\pi_X D_{MAX,19}(1+r_D) + (1-\pi_X)X_p}{1+r_z}$$

$$= \frac{\pi_X X_o + (1-\pi_X)X_p}{1+r_z} = V_X.$$

In case 20, $D(1+r_z) \leqslant X_p \leqslant X_o$, and D can be increased until case 19 is obtained.

Summarizing, for a firm with $NPV_A \leqslant 0$, debt capacity is V_X and occurs in case 16, 17, or 19. For a firm with $NPV_A > 0$, debt capacity is $D_{MAX,9-10}$ (case 9, 10) or $D_{MAX,11}$ (case 11). Finally, consider whether case 9, 10, or 11 is obtained for the $NPV_A > 0$ firm.

In case 11, $D_{MAX,11} \cdot r_{D_{MAX,11}} + A \leqslant X_p$. Substituting for $r_{D_{MAX,11}}$,

$$D_{MAX,11}\left(\frac{X_o(1-T) + AT - D_{MAX,11}}{D_{MAX,11}(1-T)}\right) + A \leqslant X_p$$

$$\Rightarrow (X_o - X_p)(1-T) \leqslant D_{MAX,11} - A.$$

Substituting for $D_{MAX,11}$,

$$(X_o - X_p)(1-T) \leqslant \frac{E^{\pi_X}(\tilde{X}) + \frac{AT}{1-T} + (1-\pi_X)(X_o-X_p)T}{1+r_z+\frac{T}{1-T}} - A.$$

Hence

$$(X_o - X_p)\left(1 - T + \frac{\pi_X T}{1-T}\right) \leqslant \frac{E^{\pi_X}(\tilde{X})}{1+r_z} - A = NPV_A.$$

In cases 9 and 10, $X_{\mathrm{p}} < D_{MAX,9-10} \cdot r_{D_{MAX,9-10}} + A$. Substituting for $r_{D_{MAX,9-10}}$,

$$X_{\mathrm{p}} < D_{MAX,9-10} \left(\frac{X_{\mathrm{o}}(1-T) + AT - D_{MAX,9-10}}{D_{MAX,9-10}(1-T)} \right) + A$$
$$\Rightarrow D_{MAX,9-10} - A < (X_{\mathrm{o}} - X_{\mathrm{p}})(1-T).$$

Substituting for $D_{MAX,9-10}$,

$$\frac{E^{\pi_X}(\tilde{X}) + \frac{\pi_X AT}{1-T}}{1 + r_z + \frac{\pi_X T}{1-T}} - A < (X_{\mathrm{o}} - X_{\mathrm{p}})(1-T).$$

Hence

$$(X_{\mathrm{o}} - X_{\mathrm{p}}) \left(1 - T + \frac{\pi_X T}{1-T} \right) > \frac{E^{\pi_X}(\tilde{X})}{1 + r_z} - A = NPV_A.$$

In summary, which D_{MAX} expression is obtained depends on the magnitude of NPV_A:

$$D_{MAX}$$
$$= \begin{cases} D_{MAX,9-10} = \dfrac{E^{\pi_X}(\tilde{X})(1-T) + \pi_X AT}{1 + r_z(1-T) - (1-\pi_X)T}, \\[2mm] \quad \text{if } 0 < NPV_A < \dfrac{((1+r_z)(1-T) + \pi_X T)(X_{\mathrm{o}} - X_{\mathrm{p}})}{1 + r_z}, \\[4mm] D_{MAX,11} = \dfrac{E^{\pi_X}(\tilde{X})(1-T) + AT + (1-\pi_X)(X_{\mathrm{o}} - X_{\mathrm{p}})T(1-T)}{1 + r_z(1-T)}, \\[2mm] \quad \text{if } \dfrac{((1+r_z)(1-T) + \pi_X T)(X_{\mathrm{o}} - X_{\mathrm{p}})}{1 + r_z} \leqslant NPV_A, \\[4mm] D_{MAX,16,17,19} = V_X, \quad \text{if } NPV_A \leqslant 0. \end{cases}$$

A.4 For an $NPV_A > 0$ Firm at Debt Capacity, $V_T > 0$

For an $NPV_A > 0$ firm at debt capacity, output exceeds available deductions in state "o" $(Dr + A < X^* = X_{\mathrm{o}})$, so taxes of

$(X_{\mathrm{o}} - Dr - A)T > 0$ are paid in that state. Since $\pi_X > 0$, we have $V_T > 0$ by Equation (11).

A.5   Sensitivity of $\mathbf{B}_i$ and β_i to an Increase in $\tilde{\Phi}_i$

If $\tilde{\Phi}_i$ is incrementally increased by $\delta > 0$ in both states,

$$\mathbf{B}_i = ((\Phi_{i,\mathrm{o}} + \delta) - (\Phi_{i,\mathrm{p}} + \delta)) \cdot \frac{\theta_i}{r_{\mathrm{e,o}} - r_{\mathrm{e,p}}} \Rightarrow \frac{\partial \mathbf{B}_i}{\partial \delta} = 0.$$

$$\beta_i = \frac{(\Phi_{i,\mathrm{o}} + \delta) - (\Phi_{i,\mathrm{p}} + \delta)}{\pi_i(\Phi_{i,\mathrm{o}} + \delta) + (1 - \pi_i)(\Phi_{i,\mathrm{p}} + \delta)} \cdot \frac{\theta_i(1 + r_z)}{r_{\mathrm{e,o}} - r_{\mathrm{e,p}}}$$

$$\Rightarrow \frac{\partial \beta_i}{\partial \delta} = \frac{-(\Phi_{i,\mathrm{o}} - \Phi_{i,\mathrm{p}})}{(\pi_i(\Phi_{i,\mathrm{o}} + \delta) + (1 - \pi_i)(\Phi_{i,\mathrm{p}} + \delta))^2} \cdot \frac{\theta_i(1 + r_z)}{r_{\mathrm{e,o}} - r_{\mathrm{e,p}}}$$

$$\Rightarrow \mathrm{sign}\left\{ \frac{\partial \beta_i}{\partial \delta} \right\} = \mathrm{sign}\left\{ \frac{\partial \beta_i}{\partial \tilde{\Phi}_i} \right\} = -\mathrm{sign}\{(\Phi_{i,\mathrm{o}} - \Phi_{i,\mathrm{p}}) \cdot \theta_i\}.$$

If only the state "o" cash flow is incrementally increased,

$$\mathbf{B}_i = ((\Phi_{i,\mathrm{o}} + \delta) - \Phi_{i,\mathrm{p}}) \cdot \frac{\theta_i}{r_{\mathrm{e,o}} - r_{\mathrm{e,p}}} \Rightarrow \frac{\partial \mathbf{B}_i}{\partial \delta}$$

$$= \frac{\theta_i}{r_{\mathrm{e,o}} - r_{\mathrm{e,p}}} \Rightarrow \mathrm{sign}\left\{ \frac{\partial \mathbf{B}_i}{\partial \Phi_{i,\mathrm{o}}} \right\} = \mathrm{sign}\{\theta_i\}.$$

$$\beta_i = \frac{\Phi_{i,\mathrm{o}} + \delta - \Phi_{i,\mathrm{p}}}{\pi_i(\Phi_{i,\mathrm{o}} + \delta) + (1 - \pi_i)\Phi_{i,\mathrm{p}}} \cdot \frac{\theta_i(1 + r_z)}{r_{\mathrm{e,o}} - r_{\mathrm{e,p}}}$$

$$\Rightarrow \frac{\partial \beta_i}{\partial \delta} = \frac{\Phi_{i,\mathrm{p}}}{(\pi_i(\Phi_{i,\mathrm{o}} + \delta) + (1 - \pi_i)\Phi_{i,\mathrm{p}})^2} \cdot \frac{\theta_i(1 + r_z)}{r_{\mathrm{e,o}} - r_{\mathrm{e,p}}}$$

$$\Rightarrow \mathrm{sign}\left\{ \frac{\partial \beta_i}{\partial \Phi_{i,\mathrm{o}}} \right\} = \mathrm{sign}\{\Phi_{i,\mathrm{p}} \cdot \theta_i\}.$$

If only the state "p" cash flow is incrementally increased,

$$\mathbf{B}_i = (\Phi_{i,\mathrm{o}} - (\Phi_{i,\mathrm{p}} + \delta)) \cdot \frac{\theta_i}{r_{\mathrm{e,o}} - r_{\mathrm{e,p}}} \Rightarrow \frac{\partial \mathbf{B}_i}{\partial \delta}$$

$$= \frac{-\theta_i}{r_{\mathrm{e,o}} - r_{\mathrm{e,p}}} \Rightarrow \mathrm{sign}\left\{ \frac{\partial \mathbf{B}_i}{\partial \Phi_{i,\mathrm{p}}} \right\} = -\mathrm{sign}\{\theta_i\}.$$

$$\beta_i = \frac{\Phi_{i,o} - \Phi_{i,p} - \delta}{\pi_i \Phi_{i,o} + (1 - \pi_i)(\Phi_{i,p} + \delta)} \cdot \frac{\theta_i(1 + r_z)}{r_{e,o} - r_{e,p}}$$

$$\Rightarrow \frac{\partial \beta_i}{\partial \delta} = \frac{-\Phi_{i,o}}{(\pi_i \Phi_{i,o} + (1 - \pi_i)(\Phi_{i,p} + \delta))^2} \cdot \frac{\theta_i(1 + r_z)}{r_{e,o} - r_{e,p}}$$

$$\Rightarrow \operatorname{sign}\left\{\frac{\partial \beta_i}{\partial \Phi_{i,p}}\right\} = -\operatorname{sign}\{\Phi_{i,o} \cdot \theta_i\}.$$

The sensitivity of $\mathbf{B}_i$ and β_i to an increase in $\tilde{\Phi}_i$ can be summarized as follows:

Cash flow(s) incremented:	$\operatorname{sign}\left\{\dfrac{\partial \mathbf{B}_i}{\partial \tilde{\Phi}_i}\right\}$	$\operatorname{sign}\left\{\dfrac{\partial \beta_i}{\partial \tilde{\Phi}_i}\right\}$
$\Phi_{i,o}$ and $\Phi_{i,p}$	0	$-\operatorname{sign}\left\{(\Phi_o - \Phi_p) \cdot \theta_i\right\}$
$\Phi_{i,o}$ only	$\operatorname{sign}\left\{\theta_i\right\}$	$\operatorname{sign}\left\{\Phi_p \cdot \theta_i\right\}$
$\Phi_{i,p}$ only	$-\operatorname{sign}\left\{\theta_i\right\}$	$-\operatorname{sign}\left\{\Phi_o \cdot \theta_i\right\}$

For the specific case of $0 < \Phi_{i,p} < \Phi_{i,o}$, $\theta_X > 0$,

Cash flow(s) incremented:	$\operatorname{sign}\left\{\dfrac{\partial \mathbf{B}_i}{\partial \tilde{\Phi}_i}\right\}$	$\operatorname{sign}\left\{\dfrac{\partial \beta_i}{\partial \tilde{\Phi}_i}\right\}$
$\Phi_{i,o}$ and $\Phi_{i,p}$	0	$-$
$\Phi_{i,o}$ only	$+$	$+$
$\Phi_{i,p}$ only	$-$	$-$

For the specific case of $\Phi_{i,p} = 0 < \Phi_{i,o}$, $\theta_X > 0$,

Cash flow incremented:	$\operatorname{sign}\left\{\dfrac{\partial \mathbf{B}_i}{\partial \tilde{\Phi}_i}\right\}$	$\operatorname{sign}\left\{\dfrac{\partial \beta_i}{\partial \tilde{\Phi}_i}\right\}$
$\Phi_{i,o}$ only	$+$	0

Table A.1. Risk of the tax shields and claims for each pricing case (Table 3), computed using Equation (12) and the output apportionment formulas (Table 2).

Depreciation tax shield (NTS)

Description (cases)	β_{NTS}	$\text{sign}\left\{\dfrac{\partial \beta_{NTS}}{\partial D}\right\}$
NTS fully used in both states (3, 4, 6–8, 10–12, 15, 17, 18)	0	0
NTS fully used in state "o," partially used in state "p" (1, 2, 5, 9, 13, 14, 16)	$\dfrac{A - X_{\mathrm{p}}}{\pi_X A + (1 - \pi_X) X_{\mathrm{p}}} \cdot \dfrac{\theta_X \cdot (1 + r_z)}{r_{e,\mathrm{o}} - r_{e,\mathrm{p}}}$	0
NTS partially used in both states (19, 20)	$\dfrac{X_{\mathrm{o}} - X_{\mathrm{p}}}{E^{\pi_X}(\tilde{X})} \cdot \dfrac{\theta_X \cdot (1 + r_z)}{r_{e,\mathrm{o}} - r_{e,\mathrm{p}}} = \beta_X$	0

Debt tax shield (DTS)

Description (cases)	β_{DTS}	$\text{sign}\left\{\dfrac{\partial \beta_{DTS}}{\partial D}\right\}$
DTS fully used in both states (4, 8, 11, 12)	0	0
DTS partially used in state "o," zero in state "p" (1, 2, 5, 9, 13, 14, 16)	$\dfrac{1}{\pi_X} \cdot \dfrac{\theta_X \cdot (1 + r_z)}{r_{e,\mathrm{o}} - r_{e,\mathrm{p}}}$	0
DTS partially used in both states (15, 17, 18)	$\dfrac{X_{\mathrm{o}} - X_{\mathrm{p}}}{E^{\pi_X}(\tilde{X}) - A} \cdot \dfrac{\theta_X \cdot (1 + r_z)}{r_{e,\mathrm{o}} - r_{e,\mathrm{p}}}$	0
DTS fully used in state "o," partially used in state "p"; debt riskless (3, 7)	$\dfrac{r_z D - (X_{\mathrm{p}} - A)}{\pi_X r_z D + (1 - \pi_X)(X_{\mathrm{p}} - A)} \cdot \dfrac{\theta_X \cdot (1 + r_z)}{r_{e,\mathrm{o}} - r_{e,\mathrm{p}}}$	$\text{sign}\{\theta_X\}$

(Continued)

Table A.1. (*Continued*)

Description (cases)	β_{NTS}	$\text{sign}\left\{\dfrac{\partial \beta_{NTS}}{\partial D}\right\}$
DTS fully used in state "o," partially used in state "p"; debt risky (6, 10)	$\dfrac{r_D D - (X_p - A)}{\pi_X r_D D + (1-\pi_X)(X_p - A)} \cdot \dfrac{\theta_X \cdot (1+r_z)}{r_{e,o} - r_{e,p}}$	$\text{sign}\{\theta_X\}$
DTS zero in both sates (19, 20)	Null	Null

Total tax shield (*TTS*)

Description (cases)	β_{TTS}	$\text{sign}\left\{\dfrac{\partial \beta_{TTS}}{\partial D}\right\}$
TTS fully used in both states (4, 8, 11, 12)	0	0
TTS partially used in both states (13–20)	$\dfrac{X_o - X_p}{E^{\pi_X}(\tilde{X})} \cdot \dfrac{\theta_X \cdot (1+r_z)}{r_{e,o} - r_{e,p}} = \beta_X$	0
TTS fully utilized in state "o," partially in state "p"; debt risky (1, 5, 6, 9, 10)	$\dfrac{A + r_D D - X_p}{\pi_X(A + r_D D) + (1-\pi_X)X_p} \cdot \dfrac{\theta_X \cdot (1+r_z)}{r_{e,o} - r_{e,p}}$	$\text{sign}\{\theta_X\}$
TTS fully utilized in state "o," partially in state "p"; debt riskless (2, 3, 7)	$\dfrac{A + r_z D - X_p}{\pi_X(A + r_z D) + (1-\pi_X)X_p} \cdot \dfrac{\theta_X \cdot (1+r_z)}{r_{e,o} - r_{e,p}}$	$\text{sign}\{\theta_X\}$

(*Continued*)

Table A.1.   (*Continued*)

Tax claim (T)

Description (cases)	β_T	$\text{sign}\left\{\dfrac{\partial \beta_T}{\partial D}\right\}$
Taxes paid in both states; debt riskless (4, 8, 12)	$\dfrac{X_o - X_p}{E^{\pi_X}(\tilde{X}) - (A + r_z D)} \cdot \dfrac{\theta_X \cdot (1+r_z)}{r_{e,o} - r_{e,p}}$	$\text{sign}\{\theta_X\}$
Taxes paid in both states; debt risky (11)	$\dfrac{X_o - X_p}{E^{\pi_X}(\tilde{X}) - (A + r_{11}D)} \cdot \dfrac{\theta_X \cdot (1+r_z)}{r_{e,o} - r_{e,p}}$	$\text{sign}\{\theta_X\}$
Taxes paid in state "o" but not in state "p" (1–3, 5–7, 9, 10)	$\dfrac{1}{\pi_X} \cdot \dfrac{\theta_X \cdot (1+r_z)}{r_{e,o} - r_{e,p}}$	0
Zero tax paid in both states (13–20)	Null	Null

Debt claim (D)

Description (cases)	β_D	$\text{sign}\left\{\dfrac{\partial \beta_D}{\partial D}\right\}$
Riskless debt (2–4, 7, 8, 12, 14, 15, 18, 20)	0	0
Default in state "p"; no tax paid in state "p" (1, 5, 6, 9, 10, 13, 16, 17, 19)	$\dfrac{D(1+r_D) - X_p}{\pi_X D(1+r_D) + (1-\pi_X)X_p} \cdot \dfrac{\theta_X \cdot (1+r_z)}{r_{e,o} - r_{e,p}}$	$\text{sign}\{\theta_X\}$
Default in state "p," taxes paid in state "p" (11)	$\dfrac{D(1+r_{11}) - (X_p(1-T) + (A + r_{11}D)T)}{\pi_X D(1+r_{11}) + (1-\pi_X)(X_p(1-T) + (A + r_{11}D)T)} \cdot \dfrac{\theta_X \cdot (1+r_z)}{r_{e,o} - r_{e,p}}$	$\text{sign}\{\theta_X\}$

(*Continued*)

Table A.1. (*Continued*)

Equity claim (E)		
Description (cases)	β_E	sign$\left\{\dfrac{\partial\beta_E}{\partial D}\right\}$
Equity flow zero in state "p"; risky debt (1, 5, 6, 9–11, 13, 16, 17, 19)	$\dfrac{1}{\pi_X}\cdot\dfrac{\theta_X\cdot(1+r_z)}{r_{e,o}-r_{e,p}}$	0
Taxes paid in state "o" but not in state "p"; riskless debt (2, 3, 7)	$\dfrac{X_o(1-T)+(A+Dr_z)T-X_p}{\pi_X(X_o(1-T)+AT-D(1+r_z(1-T)))+(1-\pi_X)(X_p-D(1+r_z))}\cdot\dfrac{\theta_X\cdot(1+r_z)}{r_{e,o}-r_{e,p}}$	sign$\{\theta_X\}$
Taxes paid in both states; riskless debt (4, 8, 12)	$\dfrac{X_o-X_p}{E^{\pi_X}(\tilde{X})+\frac{AT}{1-T}-\frac{D(1+r_z(1-T))}{1-T}}\cdot\dfrac{\theta_X\cdot(1+r_z)}{r_{e,o}-r_{e,p}}$	sign$\{\theta_X\}$
No taxes paid; riskless debt (14, 15, 18, 20)	$\dfrac{X_o-X_p}{E^{\pi_X}(\tilde{X})-D(1+r_z)}\cdot\dfrac{\theta_X\cdot(1+r_z)}{r_{e,o}-r_{e,p}}$	sign$\{\theta_X\}$

(*Continued*)

Table A.1.   (*Continued*)

Levered firm $(D+E)$

Description (cases)	β_{D+E}	$\text{sign}\left\{\dfrac{\partial \beta_{D+E}}{\partial D}\right\}$
TTS riskless, fully used in both states; riskless debt (4, 8, 12)	$\dfrac{X_o - X_p}{E^{\pi_X}(\tilde{X}) + \frac{(A+Dr_z)T}{1-T}} \cdot \dfrac{\theta_X \cdot (1+r_z)}{r_{e,o} - r_{e,p}}$	$-\text{sign}\{\theta_X\}$
TTS riskless, fully used in both states; risky debt (11)	$\dfrac{X_o - X_p}{E^{\pi_X}(\tilde{X}) + \frac{(A+Dr_{11})T}{1-T}} \cdot \dfrac{\theta_X \cdot (1+r_z)}{r_{e,o} - r_{e,p}}$	$-\text{sign}\{\theta_X\}$
TTS risky, fully used in state "o," partially used in state "p"; risky debt (1, 5, 6, 9, 10)	$\dfrac{X_o(1-T) + (A+Dr_D)T - X_p}{\pi_X(X_o(1-T) + (A+Dr_D)T) + (1-\pi_X)X_p} \cdot \dfrac{\theta_X \cdot (1+r_z)}{r_{e,o} - r_{e,p}}$	$\text{sign}\{\theta_X\}$
TTS risky, fully used in state "o," partially used in state "p"; riskless debt (2, 3, 7)	$\dfrac{X_o(1-T) + (A+Dr_z)T - X_p}{\pi_X(X_o(1-T) + (A+Dr_z)T) + (1-\pi_X)X_p} \cdot \dfrac{\theta_X \cdot 1 + r_z)}{r_{e,o} - r_{e,p}}$	$\text{sign}\{\theta_X\}$
TTS risky, partially used in both states (13–20)	$\dfrac{X_o - X_p}{E^{\pi_X}(\tilde{X})} \cdot \dfrac{\theta_X \cdot (1+r_z)}{r_{e,o} - r_{e,p}} = \beta_X$	0

(*Continued*)

Table A.1.   (*Continued*)

Unlevered firm (U)	
Description (cases*)	β^U
NTS fully used in both states (3, 4, 6–8, 10–12, 15, 17, 18)	$\dfrac{X_{\mathrm{o}} - X_{\mathrm{p}}}{E^{\pi_X}(\tilde{X}) + \frac{AT}{1-T}} \cdot \dfrac{\theta_X \cdot (1+r_z)}{r_{e,\mathrm{o}} - r_{e,\mathrm{p}}}$
NTS fully used in state "o," partially used in state "p" (1, 2, 5, 9, 13, 14, 16)	$\dfrac{X_{\mathrm{o}}(1-T) + AT - X_{\mathrm{p}}}{\pi_X\left(X_{\mathrm{o}}(1-T) + AT\right) + (1-\pi_X)X_{\mathrm{p}}} \cdot \dfrac{\theta_X \cdot (1+r_z)}{r_{e,\mathrm{o}} - r_{e,\mathrm{p}}}$
NTS partially used in both states (19, 20)	$\dfrac{X_{\mathrm{o}} - X_{\mathrm{p}}}{E^{\pi_X}(\tilde{X})} \cdot \dfrac{\theta_X \cdot (1+r_z)}{r_{e,\mathrm{o}} - r_{e,\mathrm{p}}} = \beta_X$

*Unlevered firm risk, β^U, depends only on A and $\tilde{X}$; D and r are irrelevant. Case numbers here are for an otherwise identical but levered firm.

Table A.2. Post-financing expected MTR computed as the expected value of the applicable tax rate (tax payment divided by pre-tax income). Since we assume a flat statutory tax rate of 30%, the tax rate paid on taxable income is either 30% or zero.

	Debt amount (D)						
2×2 example	0	40,000	46,296.30	80,000	100,000	105,000	$D_{MAX} =$ 110,661.75
Tax rate, state "o"	0.3	0.3	0.3	0.3	0.3	0.3	0.3
Tax rate, state "p"	0	0	0	0	0	0	0
E(tax rate) $= MTR$	0.255	0.255	0.255	0.255	0.255	0.255	0.255
5×5 example	0	40,000	76,716.29	80,000	100,000	105,000	113,108.40
Tax rate, state 1	0.3	0.3	0.3	0.3	0.3	0.3	0.3
Tax rate, state 2	0.3	0.3	0.3	0.3	0.3	0.3	0
Tax rate, state 3	0.3	0.3	0.3	0.3	0.3	0.3	0
Tax rate, state 4	0.3	0.3	0.3	0.3	0.3	0	0
Tax rate, state 5	0	0	0	0	0	0	0
E(tax rate) $= MTR$	0.2317	0.2317	0.2317	0.2317	0.2317	0.1772	0.0683

Appendix B

Examples Illustrating the Firm's Balance Sheet Using the Data in Table 8

Table B.1. Results for the 2×2 example, for seven debt levels. The debt is risky when $D > \$46{,}296.30$.

				Debt amount (D)			
	0	40,000	46,296.30	80,000	100,000	105,000	$D_{MAX} =$ 110,661.75
Pricing case (Table 3)	2	2	1	1	5	9	9
Debt							
$\Phi_{D,o}$	0	43,200.00	50,000.00	99,970.39	129,623.15	137,036.34	145,430.66
$\Phi_{D,p}$	0	43,200.00	50,000.00	50,000.00	50,000.00	50,000.00	50,000.00
$E(\Phi_D)$	0	43,200.00	50,000.00	92,474.83	117,679.68	123,980.89	131,116.06
β_D	Null	0	0	1.898	2.420	2.519	2.621
k_D	0.08	0.08	0.08	0.1559	0.1768	0.1808	0.1848
V_D	0	40,000	46,296.30	80,000	100,000	105,000	110,661.75
Par yield, r	0.08	0.08	0.08	0.2496	0.2962	0.3051	0.3142
Promised pmt, $D(1+r)$	0	43,200.00	50,000.01	99,970.39	129,623.15	137,036.34	145,430.66
Debt tax shield							
$\Phi_{DTS,o}$	0	960.00	1,111.11	5,991.12	8,886.94	9,610.90	10,430.67
$\Phi_{DTS,p}$	0	0	0	0	0	0	0
$E(\Phi_{DTS})$	0	816.00	944.44	5,092.45	7,553.90	8,169.27	8,866.07
β_{DTS}	Null	4.506	4.506	4.506	4.506	4.506	4.506
k_{DTS}	0.08	0.2602	0.2602	0.2602	0.2602	0.2602	0.2602
V_{DTS}	0	647.49	749.42	4,040.85	5,994.01	6,482.30	7,035.21

(Continued)

Table B.1. (*Continued*)

			Debt amount (D)				
	0	40,000	46,296.30	80,000	100,000	105,000	$D_{MAX} =$ 110,661.75
Depreciation tax shield (for any feasible D)							
$\Phi_{NTS,o}$	30,000.00						
$\Phi_{NTS,p}$	15,000.00						
$E(\Phi_{NTS})$	27,750.00						
β_{NTS}	1.899						
k_{NTS}	0.1560						
V_{NTS}	24,005.99						
Total tax shield							
$\Phi_{TTS,o}$	30,000.00	30,960.00	31,111.11	35,991.12	38,886.94	39,610.90	40,430.67
$\Phi_{TTS,p}$	15,000.00	15,000.00	15,000.00	15,000.00	15,000.00	15,000.00	15,000.00
$E(\tilde{\Phi})$	27,750.00	28,566.00	28,694.44	32,842.45	35,303.90	35,919.27	36,616.07
β_{TTS}	1.899	1.968	1.978	2.275	2.420	2.453	2.490
k_{TTS}	0.1560	0.1587	0.1591	0.1710	0.1768	0.1781	0.1796
V_{TTS}	24,005.99	24,653.49	24,755.41	28,046.84	30,000.00	30,488.29	31,041.20
Taxes							
$\Phi_{T,o}$	15,000.00	14,040.00	13,888.89	9,008.88	6,113.06	5,389.10	4,569.33
$\Phi_{T,p}$	0	0	0	0	0	0	0
$E(\tilde{\Phi})$	12,750.00	11,934.00	11,805.56	7,657.55	5,196.10	4,580.73	3,883.93
β_T	4.506	4.506	4.506	4.506	4.506	4.506	4.506
k_T	0.2602	0.2602	0.2602	0.2602	0.2602	0.2602	0.2602
V_T	10,117.10	9,469.61	9,367.69	6,076.25	4,123.09	3,634.80	3,081.89

(*Continued*)

Table B.1. (Continued)

	\multicolumn{7}{c}{Debt amount (D)}
	0	40,000	46,296.30	80,000	100,000	105,000	$D_{MAX} =$ 110,661.75
Equity							
$\Phi_{E,o}$	135,000.00	92,760.00	86,111.11	41,020.73	14,263.80	7,574.56	0.01
$\Phi_{E,p}$	50,0000.00	6,800.00	0	0	0	0	0
$E(\tilde{\Phi}_E)$	$122,250.00 = E(\tilde{\Phi}^U)$	79,866.00	73,194.44	34,867.62	12,124.23	6,438.38	0.01
β_E	$2.493 = \beta^U$	4.065	4.506	4.506	4.506	4.506	4.506
k_E	$0.1797 = k^U$	0.2426	0.2602	0.2602	0.2602	0.2602	0.2602
V_E	$103,626.54 = V^U$	64,274.04	58,079.66	27,667.39	9,620.55	5,108.84	0.01
E_0	100,000.00	60,000.00	53,703.70	20,000.00	0	0	0
Wealth gain, ΔW	3,626.54	4,274.04	4,375.96	7,667.39	9,620.55	10,108.84	10,661.76
DIV_0	0	0	0	0	0	5,000.00	10,661.75
Debt + equity							
$\Phi_{D+E,o}$	135,000.00	135,960.00	136,111.11	140,991.12	143,886.94	144,610.90	145,430.67
$\Phi_{D+E,p}$	50,0000.00	50,000.00	50,000.00	50,000.00	50,000.00	50,000.00	50,000.00
$E(\tilde{\Phi}_{D+E})$	122,250.00	123,066.00	123,194.44	127,342.45	129,803.90	130,419.27	131,116.07
β_{D+E}	2.493	2.505	2.507	2.568	2.603	2.611	2.621
$k_{D+E} = WACC$	0.1797	0.1802	0.1803	0.1827	0.1841	0.1845	0.1848
$V_{D+E} = V^L$	103,626.54	104,274.04	104,375.96	107,667.39	109,620.55	110,108.84	110,661.76
Debt + equity + tax (for any feasible D)							
$\Phi_{D+E+T,o}$	150,000.00						
$\Phi_{D+E+T,p}$	50,0000.00						
$E(\tilde{\Phi}_{D+E+T})$	135,000.00						
β_{D+E+T}	2.672						
k_{D+E+T}	0.1869						
V_{D+E+T}	113,743.65						

Table B.2. Results for the 5 × 5 example, for seven debt levels. The debt is risky when D >$76,716.29.

				Debt amount (D)			
	0	40,000	76,716.29	80,000	100,000	105,000	$D_{MAX} =$ 113,108.40
Debt							
$\Phi_{D,1}$	0	43,200.00	82,853.60	88,173.63	120,576.27	130,728.00	181,528.35
$\Phi_{D,2}$	0	43,200.00	82,853.60	88,173.63	120,576.27	130,728.00	145,005.02
$\Phi_{D,3}$	0	43,200.00	82,853.60	88,173.63	120,576.27	130,728.00	135,000.00
$\Phi_{D,4}$	0	43,200.00	82,853.60	88,173.63	120,576.27	124,994.98	124,994.98
$\Phi_{D,5}$	0	43,200.00	82,853.60	82,853.60	82,853.60	82,853.60	82,853.60
$E(\tilde\Phi_D)$	0	43,200.00	82,853.60	86,961.95	111,984.59	118,783.66	133,720.44
β_D	Null	0	0	0.176	0.996	1.282	2.556
k_D	0.08	0.08	0.08	0.0870	0.1198	0.1313	0.1822
V_D	0	40,000	76,716.29	80,000	100,000	105,000	113,108.40
Par yield, r	0.08	0.08	0.08	0.1022	0.2058	0.2450	0.6049
Promised pmt, $D(1+r)$	0	43,200.00	82,853.60	88,173.63	120,576.27	130,728.00	181,528.35
Debt tax shield							
$\phi_{DTS,1}$	0	960.00	1,841.19	2,452.09	6,172.88	7,718.40	20,525.99
$\Phi_{DTS,2}$	0	960.00	1,841.19	2,452.09	6,172.88	7,718.40	13,501.51
$\Phi_{DTS,3}$	0	960.00	1,841.19	2,452.09	6,172.88	7,718.40	10,500.00
$\Phi_{DTS,4}$	0	960.00	1,841.19	2,452.09	6,172.88	7,498.49	7,498.49
$\Phi_{DTS,5}$	0	0	0	0	0	0	0
$E(\tilde\Phi_{DTS})$	0	71.35	1,421.84	1,893.60	4,766.95	8,169.27	10,392.04
β_{DTS}	Null	4.278	4.278	4.278	4.278	4.389	8.599
k_{DTS}	Null	0.2511	0.2511	0.2511	0.2511	0.2556	0.4240
V_{DTS}	0	592.54	1,136.45	1,513.51	3,810.11	4,715.50	7,297.92

(*Continued*)

Table B.2. (Continued)

				Debt amount (D)			
	0	40,000	76,716.29	80,000	100,000	105,000	$D_{MAX} =$ 113,108.40
Depreciation tax shield (for any feasible D)							
$\Phi_{NTS,1}$	30,000.00						
$\Phi_{NTS,2}$	30,000.00						
$\Phi_{NTS,3}$	30,000.00						
$\Phi_{NTS,4}$	30,000.00						
$\Phi_{NTS,5}$	24,856.08						
$E(\bar{\Phi}_{NTS})$	28,828.43						
β_{NTS}	0.519						
k_{NTS}	0.1007						
V_{NTS}	26,189.89						
Total tax shield							
$\Phi_{TTS,1}$	30,000.00	30,960.00	31,841.19	32,452.09	36,172.88	37,718.40	50,525.99
$\Phi_{TTS,2}$	30,000.00	30,960.00	31,841.19	32,452.09	36,172.88	37,718.40	43,501.51
$\Phi_{TTS,3}$	30,000.00	30,960.00	31,841.19	32,452.09	36,172.88	37,718.40	40,500.00
$\Phi_{TTS,4}$	30,000.00	30,960.00	31,841.19	32,452.09	36,172.88	37,498.49	37,498.49
$\Phi_{TTS,5}$	24,856.08	24,856.08	24,856.08	24,856.08	24,856.08	24,856.08	24,856.08
$E(\bar{\Phi}_{TTS})$	28,828.43	29,569.78	30,250.27	30,722.03	33,595.38	34,748.98	39,220.46
β_{TTS}	0.519	0.602	0.675	0.724	0.996	1.109	2.280
k_{TTS}	0.1007	0.1041	0.1070	0.1090	0.1198	0.1244	0.1712
V_{TTS}	26,189.89	26,782.43	27,326.34	27,703.40	30,000.00	30,905.39	33,487.81

(Continued)

Table B.2. *(Continued)*

	Debt amount (D)						
	0	40,000	76,716.29	80,000	100,000	105,000	$D_{MAX} =$ 113,108.40
Taxes							
$\Phi_{T,1}$	26,143.92	25,183.92	24,302.73	23,691.83	19,971.04	18,425.52	5,617.93
$\Phi_{T,2}$	13,501.51	12,541.51	11,660.32	11,049.42	7,328.63	5,783.11	0
$\Phi_{T,3}$	10,500.00	9,540.00	8,658.81	8,047.91	4,327.12	2,781.60	0
$\Phi_{T,4}$	7,498.49	6,538.49	5,657.30	5,046.40	1,325.61	0	0
$\Phi_{T,5}$	0	0	0	0	0	0	0
$E(\tilde{\Phi}_T)$	11,671.57	10,930.22	10,249.73	9,777.97	6,904.62	5,751.02	1,279.54
β_T	9.781	10.225	10.701	11.078	14.865	17.682	23.352
k_T	0.4712	0.4890	0.5080	0.5231	0.6746	0.7873	1.0141
V_T	7,933.22	7,340.68	6,796.78	6,419.71	4,123.11	3,217.73	635.30
Equity							
$\Phi_{E,1}$	161,002.48	118,762.48	79,990.08	75,280.94	46,599.10	37,992.88	0.12
$\Phi_{E,2}$	131,503.51	89,263.51	50,491.11	45,781.97	17,100.13	8,493.91	0
$\Phi_{E,3}$	124,500.00	82,260.00	43,487.59	38,778.46	10,096.61	1,490.40	0
$\Phi_{E,4}$	117,496.49	75,256.49	36,484.08	31,774.94	3,093.10	0	0
$\Phi_{E,5}$	82,853.60	39,653.60	0	0	0	0	0
$E(\tilde{\Phi}_E)$	$123,328.43 = E(\tilde{\Phi}^U)$	80,869.78	41,896.67	34,867.62	16,110.79	10,465.32	0.03
β_E	$2.139 = \beta^U$	3.447	7.648	8.006	14.865	20.346	23.352
k_E	$0.1656 = k^U$	0.2179	0.3859	0.4002	0.6746	0.8938	1.0141
V_E	$105,810.48 = V^U$	66,403.03	30,230.64	27,324.00	9,620.59	5,525.98	0.01
E_0	100,000.00	60,000.00	23,283.71	20,000.00	0	0	0
Wealth gain, ΔW	5,810.48	6,403.03	6,946.93	7,324.00	9,620.59	10,525.98	13,108.41
DIV_0	0	0	0	0	0	5,000.00	13,108.40

(Continued)

Table B.2.   (Continued)

				Debt amount (D)			
	0	40,000	76,716.29	80,000	100,000	105,000	$D_{MAX} =$ 113,108.40
Debt + equity							
$\bar{\Phi}_{D+E,1}$	161,002.48	161,962.48	162,843.67	163,454.57	167,175.36	168,720.88	181,528.47
$\Phi_{D+E,2}$	131,503.51	132,463.51	133,344.71	133,955.60	137,676.39	139,221.91	145,005.02
$\Phi_{D+E,3}$	124,500.00	125,460.00	126,341.19	126,952.09	130,672.88	132,218.40	135,000.00
$\Phi_{D+E,4}$	117,496.49	118,456.49	119,337.68	119,948.58	123,669.37	124,994.98	124,994.98
$\Phi_{D+E,5}$	82,853.60	82,853.60	82,853.60	82,853.60	82,853.60	82,853.60	82,853.60
$E(\bar{\Phi}_{D+E})$	123,328.43	124,069.78	124,750.27	125,222.03	128,095.38	130,419.27	133,720.46
β_{D+E}	2.139	2.151	2.162	2.169	2.213	2.235	2.556
$k_{D+E} = WACC$	0.1656	0.1660	0.1665	0.1668	0.1685	0.1694	0.1822
$V_{D+E} = V^L$	105,810.48	106,403.03	106,946.93	107,324.00	109,620.59	110,525.98	113,108.41

Debt + equity + tax (for any feasible D)

$\Phi_{D+E+T,1}$	187,146.40
$\Phi_{D+E+T,2}$	145,005.20
$\Phi_{D+E+T,3}$	135,000.00
$\Phi_{D+E+T,4}$	124,994.98
$\Phi_{D+E+T,5}$	82,853.60
$E(\bar{\Phi}_{D+E+T})$	135,000.00
β_{D+E+T}	2.672
k_{D+E+T}	0.1869
V_{D+E+T}	113,743.71

References

Auerbach, AJ (1983). Taxation, corporate financial policy and the cost of capital. *Journal of Economic Literature*, 21(3), 905–940.

Auerbach, AJ and K Hassett (1992). Tax policy and business fixed investment in the United States. *Journal of Public Economics*, 47(2), 141–170.

Baron, DP (1975). Firm valuation, corporate taxes and default risk. *Journal of Finance*, 30(5), 1251–1264.

Bierman, HJ (1993). Capital budgeting in 1992: A survey. *Financial Management*, 22, 22–24.

Bruner, RF, KM Eades, R Harris and RC Higgins (1998). Best practices in estimating the cost of capital: Survey and synthesis. *Financial Practice and Education*, 8, 13–28.

Brennan, M and F Schwartz (1978). Corporate income taxes, valuation and the problem of optimal capital structure. *Journal of Business*, 51(1), 103–114.

Bulow, JI and LH Summers (1984). The taxation of risky assets. *Journal of Political Economy*, 92(1), 20–39.

Caballero, RJ (1999). Aggregate investment. In *Handbook of Macroeconomics*, JB Taylor and M Woodford (eds.) (1B), pp. 813–862. Amsterdam: North Holland.

Chamberlain, G and M Rothschild (1983). Arbitrage, factor structure, and mean-variance analysis on large asset markets. *Econometrica*, 51 (September), 1281–1304.

Connor, G and RA Korazcyk (1993). A test of the number of factors in an approximate factor model. *Journal of Finance*, 48(4), 1263–1291.

Copeland, TE, T Koller and J Murrin (2000). *Valuation: Measuring and Managing the Value of Companies*, 3rd Ed. New York: Wiley.

Copeland, TE (2002). What do practitioners want? *Journal of Applied Finance*, 12(1), 5–12.

Dammon, R and LW Senbet (1988). The effects of taxes and depreciation on corporate investment and financial leverage. *Journal of Finance*, 43(2), 357–373.

DeAngelo, H and R Masulis (1980). Optimal capital structure under corporate and personal taxation. *Journal of Financial Economics*, 8(1), 3–27.

Ehrhardt, MC and PR Daves (2002). Corporate valuation: The combined impact of growth and the tax shield of debt on the cost of capital and systematic risk. *Journal of Applied Finance*, 12(2), 7–14.

Fernandez, P (2004). The value of tax shields is not equal to the present value of tax shields. *Journal of Financial Economics*, 73(1), 145–165.

Fullerton, D (1984). Which effective tax rate? *The National Tax Journal*, 28(1), 23–41.

Galai, D (1998). Taxes, M-M propositions and the government's implicit cost of capital in investment projects in the private sector. *European Financial Management*, 4(2), 143–157.

Galai, D and RW Masulis (1976). The option pricing model and the risk factor of stock. *Journal of Financial Economics*, 3(1/2), 53–81.

Gonzales, N, R Litzenberger and J Rolfo (1977). On mean variance models of capital structure and the absurdity of their predications. *Journal of Financial and Quantitative Analysis*, 12(2), 165–179.

Graham, JR (1996a). Debt and the marginal tax rate. *Journal of Financial Economics*, 41, 41–73.

Graham, JR (1996b). Proxies for the corporate marginal tax rate. *Journal of Financial Economics*, 42, 187–221.

Graham, JR (2000). How big are the tax benefits of debt? *Journal of Finance*, 55(October), 1901–1941.

Graham, JR and CR Harvey (2001). The theory and practice of corporate finance: Evidence from the field. *Journal of Financial Economics*, 60, 187–243.

Graham, JR and ML Lemmon (1998). Measuring corporate tax rates and tax incentives: A new approach. *Journal of Applied Corporate Finance*, 11(Spring) 54–65.

Green, RC and E Talmor (1985). The structure and incentive effects of corporate tax liabilities. *Journal of Finance*, 40(4), 1095–1114.

Grinblatt, M and S Titman (1983). Factor pricing in a finite economy. *Journal of Financial Economics*, 12, 497–507.

Grinblatt, M and S Titman (2002). *Financial Markets and Corporate Strategy*, 2nd Ed. Irwin: McGraw-Hill.

Grinblatt, M and S Titman (1985). Approximate factor structures: Interpretations and implications for empirical tests. *Journal of Finance*, 40(5), 1367–1373.

Hamada, RS (1969). Portfolio analysis, market equilibrium and corporate finance. *Journal of Finance*, 24(1), 13–31.

Harris, RS and JJ Pringle (1985). Risk adjusted discount rates: Extensions from the average risk case. *Journal of Financial Research*, 8(Fall), 237–244.

Hite, GL (1977). Leverage, output effects and the M-M theorems. *Journal of Financial Economics*, 4(2), 177–202.

Kaplan, SN and R Ruback. (1995). The valuation of cash flow forecasts: An empirical analysis. *Journal of Finance*, 50(4), 1959–1093.

Kim, EH (1978). A mean-variance theory of optimal capital structure and corporate debt capacity. *Journal of Finance*, 33(1), 45–63.

Kraus, A and RH Litzenberger (1973). A state preference model of optimal financial leverage. *Journal of Finance*, 28(September), 911–922.

Lau, LJ (2000). *Econometrics: Econometrics and the Cost of Capital*, Vol. 2. Cambridge, MA: MIT Press.

Leland, HE (1994). Corporate debt value, bond covenants, and optimal capital structure. *Journal of Finance*, 49(4), 1213–1252.

Lewis, CM (1990). A multiperiod theory of corporate financial policy under taxation. *Journal of Financial and Quantitative Analysis*, 25(March), 25–42.

Long, JB (1974). Discussion. *Journal of Finance*, 29, 485–488.

Mackie-Mason, JK (1990). Do taxes affect corporate financing decisions? *Journal of Finance*, 45(5), 1471–1493.

Majd, S and SC Myers (1985). Valuing the government's tax claim on risky corporate assets. NBER Working Paper 1553, Cambridge, MA.

Mauer, D and A Triantis (1994). Interactions of corporate financing and investment decisions: A dynamic framework. *Journal of Finance*, 49, 1253–1277.

Merton, RC (1974). On the pricing of corporate debt: The risk structure of interest rates. *Journal of Finance*, 29(2), 449–470.

Miles, J and J Ezzell (1980). The weighted average cost of capital, perfect capital markets, and project life: A clarification. *Journal of Financial and Quantitative Analysis*, 15(September), 719–730.

Miles, J and J Ezzell (1985). Reformulating tax shield valuation: A note. *Journal of Finance*, 40, 1485–1492.

Miller, MH (1988). The Modigliani–Miller propositions after thirty years. *Journal of Economic Perspectives*, 2(4), 99–120.

Miller, MH (1977). Debt and taxes. *Journal of Finance*, 32(2), 261–275.

Modigliani, F (1988). MM-past, present and future. *Journal of Economic Perspectives*, 2(4), 149–158.

Modigliani, F and MH Miller (1958). The cost of capital, corporation finance and the theory of investment. *American Economic Review*, 48(3), 261–297.

Modigliani, F and MH Miller (1963). Corporate income taxes and the cost of capital: A correction. *American Economic Review*, 53(3), 433–443.

Myers, SC (1974). Interactions of corporate financing and investment decisions: Implications for capital budgeting. *Journal of Finance*, 29(1), 1–25.

Myers, SC (1977). The determinants of corporate borrowing. *Journal of Financial Economics*, 5(2), 147–175.

Reinschmidt, KF (2002). Aggregate social discount rate derived from individual discount rates. *Management Science*, 48, 307–312.

Rosen, HS (1998). Do taxes affect entrepreneurs' investments? 41st Alex G. McKenna Economic Education Series Lecture, March 1998.

Ross, SA (1976). The arbitrage theory of capital asset prices. *Journal of Economic Theory*, 13(3), 341–360.

Ross, SA (1987). Arbitrage and martingales with taxation. *Journal of Political Economy*, 95(2), 371–392.

Ross, SA (1985). Debt and taxes under uncertainty. *Journal of Finance*, 40, 637–657.

Ross, SA, R Westerfield and JF Jaffe (1988). *Corporate Finance*, 6th Ed. Homewood, IL: Irwin.

Ruback, RS (2002). Capital cash flows: A simple approach to valuing risky cash flows. *Financial Management*, Summer, 85–103.

Rubinstein, M (1973). A mean-variance synthesis of corporate financial theory. *Journal of Finance*, 28(1), 167–181.

Scholes, M and M Wolfson (1992). *Taxes and Business Strategy*. Englewood Cliffs, NJ: Prentice-Hall.

Taggart, RA (1991). Consistent valuation and cost of capital expressions with corporate and personal taxes. *Financial Management*, Autumn, 8–20.

Talmor, E, R Haugen and A Barnea (1985). The value of the tax subsidy on risky debt. *Journal of Business*, 58(2), 191–202.

Turnbull, SM (1979). Debt capacity. *Journal of Finance*, 34, 931–940.

Zechner, J and P Swoboda (1986). The critical implicit tax rate and capital structure. *Journal of Banking and Finance*, 10, 327–341.